How to Parent Your Anxious Toddler

of related interest

The Panicosaurus
Managing Anxiety in Children
Including Those with Asperger Syndrome
K.I. Al-Ghani
Ilustrated by Haitham Al-Ghani
ISBN 978 1 84905 356 3
eISBN 978 0 85700 706 3

Can I tell you about Anxiety?
A guide for friends, family and professionals
Lucy Willetts and Polly Waite
Part of the Can I tell you about…? series
ISBN 978 1 84905 527 7
eISBN 978 0 85700 967 8

Constipation, Withholding and Your Child
A Family Guide to Soiling and Wetting
Anthony Cohn
ISBN 978 1 84310 491 9
eISBN 978 1 84642 562 2

Ready, Set, Potty!
Toilet Training for Children with Autism and
Other Developmental Disorders
Brenda Batts
ISBN 978 1 84905 833 9
eISBN 978 0 85700 310 2

Liam Goes Poo in the Toilet
A Story about Trouble with Toilet Training
Jane Whelen Banks
ISBN 978 1 84310 900 6
eISBN 978 1 84642 874 6

Attacking Anxiety
A Step-by-Step Guide to an Engaging Approach
to Treating Anxiety and Phobias in Children with
Autism and Other Developmental Disabilities
Karen Levine and Naomi Chedd
ISBN 978 1 84905 788 2
eISBN 978 1 78450 044 3

How to Parent Your Anxious Toddler

Natasha Daniels

Jessica Kingsley *Publishers*
London and Philadelphia

First published in 2016
by Jessica Kingsley Publishers
73 Collier Street
London N1 9BE, UK
and
400 Market Street, Suite 400
Philadelphia, PA 19106, USA

www.jkp.com

Library of Congress Cataloging in Publication Data
Daniels, Natasha.
  How to parent your anxious toddler / Natasha Daniels.
    pages cm
  ISBN 978-1-84905-738-7 (alk. paper)
  1. Anxiety in children. 2. Toddlers--Development. 3. Parenting. 4. Parent and
child. I. Title.
  BF723.A5D36 2016
  649'.123--dc23

                           2015016720

British Library Cataloguing in Publication Data
A CIP catalogue record for this book is available from the British Library

ISBN 978 1 84905 738 7
eISBN 978 1 78450 148 8

Printed and bound in the United States

• •

To my three children, who continually teach me more about life than anyone else and to my husband, who makes my life sparkle.

Contents

• • • • • • • • • • • • • • •

Introduction: What Does an Anxious Toddler Look Like?

Does your toddler get upset when his routine is disrupted? Does he follow you from room to room and is he unable to play on his own? Do you struggle with daily routines like mealtimes, bath time and bedtime? Sounds like most toddlers, right? Common toddler struggles are amplified for the anxious toddler. Parents are often told that their toddler is just going through their "terrible twos" or that "it's just a phase," but parents who live with an anxious toddler know that it is more than that. Being frequently woken up at all hours of the night, having two-hour meltdowns if the routine is disrupted, gagging on mixed textures and only eating a handful of food choices, and lining up toys and having a fit if someone takes one out of line—this just doesn't seem like a "typical" toddler to most parents who live with these behaviors on a daily basis!

This book is designed for parents who need support and guidance on how to parent their anxious child. Some behaviors may be confusing or misunderstood. Many typical parenting approaches don't work—or worse, make the problem bigger! Parents often feel as if they have tried everything, and nothing works. Once the toddler's behavior is demystified and explained, new effective parenting approaches can be explored. These approaches at times might seem counterintuitive to the behavior or the situation, but they can build life skills and coping mechanisms for ongoing change. The earlier parents address and treat anxiety in their child, the better the long-term outcome.

If you are reading this then you have won half the battle. You have successfully labeled your toddler's behavior as anxiety. Often in my private practice, parents will bring their older children in for anxiety issues—fears of the dark, bugs or strangers. When I ask about their history, parents will report that their child has had no prior issues with anxiety. When I ask them to describe their child when he was a toddler, I will often get the response, "Oh he was rigid, liked his routine, couldn't wear socks, was such a picky eater, was very emotional—but he didn't worry about anything back then." Parents do not always recognize that those are the early stages of anxiety. They also don't always realize that many coping mechanisms and adaptation skills can be planted at this crucial, impressionable time.

Parents often blame themselves for their child's anxiety. They wonder what they did to cause the fears and behaviors. In my practice I have worked with a large array of parents, all with varying parenting styles and approaches, and yet their anxious children all have similar behaviors and issues. Blaming yourself for your child's anxiety is not only inaccurate, but also unproductive. Often genetics, a family history of anxiety, your child's emotional sensitivity and mood issues are to blame. With that being said, parenting styles can exacerbate or minimize the level of anxiety your child will experience as they progress through childhood.

This book is divided up into chapters that explore the most common challenging areas for the anxious toddler—and their parents. Some chapters may speak to you more than others. Not every anxious child has the same struggles or behaves in the same way. Some chapters might sound as if I am describing your life, while other chapters may be completely foreign— and you will be thankful! Each chapter starts with a vignette presented through the eyes of the parent and then through the eyes of their toddler. Each vignette is a fictitious story based on common issues I have encountered and worked with in my private practice. I have worked with some wonderful families and many have understood their child's anxious behavior. However, for the sake of learning, I have highlighted in each parenting vignette the common misunderstandings and misinterpretations parents make of anxious toddler behavior. You will then get an alternative view from the toddler. You will see how the toddler views the same situation in a completely different light and why they are behaving the way they are from their perspective. Each chapter ends with various parenting approaches that help instill coping mechanisms, independence and adaptive behavior.

Toddlerhood is typically defined as the time of development between the ages of one and three. During this stage of development there is ongoing growth in your child's emotional and intellectual understanding. A toddler's language and cognitive abilities are vastly different at age one than at age three. Some children develop faster than others and may be quicker to acquire and understand language. With such an array of differences across developmental milestones between the ages of one and three, not every approach will be developmentally appropriate for your toddler. If you come across an approach that requires a higher acquisition of language or emotional maturity, make a note of the approach in case you are still dealing with that issue when your toddler is a little bit older. It is amazing how quickly toddlers change month to month! What may seem too difficult one month may be a perfect approach a few months later.

When it comes to parenting, everyone has an opinion, and some opinions can be very strong. Parents get conflicting guidance from friends, pediatricians and how-to parenting books. Different names for different parenting styles have popped up and there is an air of condemnation for those that do not do it "that way" or the "correct way!" This can make parents feel like a failure when that approach just doesn't work for their child. Every child is different, and a parenting approach might work for one child, but not another. This is definitely the case for anxious toddlers. Sometimes typical parenting approaches just don't work! Sometimes the parenting approach you have used successfully for your other children just isn't working with your anxious toddler. You have to find an approach that works best for *your* family and *your* child. This may conflict with what other people might deem to be "the right approach," but as a parent you have to make that judgement for yourself. When an approach works for your child and you feel successful as a parent, you have found the right parental approach for your child.

Throughout this book, I will frequently talk about the use of challenges and reinforcers, such as a treasure box. One of the most effective ways to eliminate your child's anxiety is by teaching them coping mechanisms and then slowly exposing them to challenging situations where they are rewarded for their progress. I will be discussing ways to present challenges to your child as we discuss specific fears and anxieties throughout this book. Children are more motivated to face their anxiety and use their coping mechanisms when there is a positive reinforcer in place, such as a trinket or a prize from a treasure box. As your child's level of anxiety improves, the use of such things as treasure boxes will decrease and eventually become completely unnecessary.

CHAPTER 1

Routine, Rigidity and Eggshells!

Carla and Tom

Carla and Tom had daily struggles with their son Sam. Carla felt as if she has to walk on eggshells all day long to avoid a complete meltdown. Carla sometimes felt trapped by Sam's behavior and moods. She felt she couldn't go out anywhere without panicking about how Sam would handle the change. She secretly got embarrassed about how her son acted around others. She couldn't help but compare Sam to other children and she felt as if no one else had to go through the struggles she had to go through. Her friends and family told her to relax and that Sam seemed "fine" to them. This only made her feel that much more alone. Tom thought Carla spoiled Sam and gave in to his every whim. Tom felt Sam didn't act that way for him and if Carla just disciplined him more, he would be a "normal" kid. Carla felt Tom didn't understand how exhausting Sam's power struggles could be.

Sometimes Carla could tell it was going to be a bad day before Sam even got fully out of bed. Sam often woke up grumpy and had a hard time in the morning. When Sam's dad accidentally bought a different brand of waffles in the morning, it took Carla two hours to calm Sam down and required Tom to make a quick trip to the store. Sam liked his waffles cut into four squares and served on his red plate. If his red plate was dirty, his mom had to hand wash it because Sam would not eat his waffles on any other plate. In the morning, they had a strict routine that seemed to comfort Sam. When Carla had a doctor's appointment or a playdate that was out of their routine, she knew Sam would have a meltdown. Sam knew most of the common routes they took in the car and when Carla made an unknown turn, Sam could instantly go into panic mode. On the flip side, when simple comments were made like, "Maybe we'll go to the park after lunch," the comments were burned into his brain and he became unglued and enraged if that activity did not occur just as he envisioned it in his mind. Carla learned to be careful with what she said in front of Sam.

Tom liked to play with Sam when he got home from work, but it always seemed to end in Sam crying. One time Tom tried to help Sam set up his trains on their train table, but unbeknownst to Tom, Sam had placed his trains in a very specific fashion. When Tom grabbed a bunch of trains to place on the bridge, Sam completely lost it. Tom got frustrated and stormed off into the other room, while Carla tried to help Sam put his trains back into the "right" position.

Sam

Sam often woke up grumpy because he didn't get enough sleep. He frequently tossed and turned, had bad dreams and woke up afraid of his shadow throughout the night. He didn't feel like talking or being nice in the mornings. Many things scared Sam and he got easily overwhelmed. The one thing he could count on was his predictable routine. He knew what to expect, how to act and what would happen in each situation. He preferred to stay at home where he felt the most comfortable.

Everything could seem daunting, even the food he ate. Once his dad brought a strange looking box of waffles instead of his trusted waffles in the yellow box. He had no idea how those waffles would taste, how they would feel in his mouth or if they might make him gag. He wondered why they would try and feed him something so strange and scary. He couldn't express his feelings so he just screamed and cried until the trusted yellow box showed back up on the counter.

He had always loved his red plate. He had never experienced bad food on his red plate so he trusted that plate. His mom always gave him the red plate, so she must have trusted it too. When his mom cut his waffle into squares, he knew it would fit perfectly in his mouth. He knew he would not not feel like he did once, when his mouth was so full from a bite he thought he would choke. He had to spit the whole mouthful out and his dad got mad at him. Sometimes he still spat out food when his mouth felt too full.

Sam has been taken to some very scary places—places with screaming kids who ran or bumped into him and made very loud noises. He once went to a place that stuck a needle in his arm and made him cry for hours. He has been to crowded places where he felt very hot and confused. He has been to places where he thought he might lose his mom if he let go of the death grip he had on her leg. So when Sam's mom took a left turn instead of the right turn she should make, Sam got into a panic. He wondered, "Where are we going? What will it be like? Will I be safe? Will it hurt my arm…my ears…?" When his mom told him they are doing something new he had many questions for her—some he didn't have the language to ask. What does it mean to go to my friend's house? Will they have strange food? Will they have loud furry things with sharp teeth that like to wet my skin and make me stink? When will I get back home? Where will I sleep?

Sometimes Sam's mom told him things and then they didn't happen. Like the time she told him they would go to the park after lunch. After lunch he got his shovel and bucket like he always did when he went to the park and his mom told him they "ran out of time." Ran out of time? They hadn't done anything else. The park was right down the road. Why did she say they were going if they weren't going to go? That's not fair! He gets in trouble when he says something that's not true so why can his mom do it? He did what he usually does when he didn't understand why he couldn't have or do something—he cried, begged and screamed. Maybe she needed to see just how upsetting this was for him! Usually if he did this for a while his mom's face would go red and then she would give him what he wants.

Sam's dad could sometimes scare him. He had a loud deep voice and sometimes it startled Sam. His dad could get upset with him easily and he didn't know why. He got put in "time out" a lot by his dad. He didn't cry as much around his dad because he was afraid to hear his loud voice. He didn't ask his dad for things as often because he thought his dad might get mad. One time his dad came home and wanted to play with Sam's trains. Sam had spent most of the day getting his trains in the "right" spot. He lined them up so that each corner was touching the corner of the next train. He also had them lined up by his favorite colors—blue…red…then green…yellow. His dad grabbed his favorite trains and took them out of order, out of color, off the corners! All he could do was scream—a very high-pitched, frantic scream! For some reason his dad began to yell at him and stormed off to another room. His mother calmed him down by hugging him tight and stroking his hair. She always did this when he was upset and it helped. She asked Sam to show him where the trains should go and he helped her line up the trains corner to corner and color to color again.

Parenting style

Carla and Tom exemplify many parents I have worked with over the years. It is common for couples to have different parenting styles. When parents approach their anxious child with vastly different parenting styles it can cause mixed messages and add further chaos to an already stressful situation.

Parents may disagree on what approach will most effectively help their child's behavior. Some parents relate more to their anxious child and may have anxiety or emotional sensitivities themselves. These parents can empathize with their child and will do whatever they need to in order to get their child to feel less anxious. They realize that their child's behaviors stem from anxiety and therefore they do not feel comfortable being strict or disciplining their behavior. Other parents have a difficult time understanding how their child's behavior is related to anxiety. Their child looks manipulative, entitled or spoiled, and the parent feels that firm discipline is what is needed to fix that behavior.

Anxious toddlers tend to do better with a "middle of the road" approach. Parents who are overly accommodating can be unknowingly enabling their child and are ironically exacerbating their child's anxiety. Children learn through this parenting style that they need to depend on their parent in order to relieve their anxiety. These children will be more likely to have separation anxiety at a later age. They adopt the misguided belief that they are not okay unless their parent is right there with them.

It is hard as a parent to sit and watch your child struggle, especially if you know exactly how to fix the problem. The issue with this approach is that you never teach your child how to problem solve or self-regulate. If you always swoop in and take on your child's pain or problem, they will never learn the skills to solve those problems themselves.

Often these parents feel their child's struggles on a deeply emotional level. They are more apt to cry with their child and to get overly involved in their child's struggles. The child feels the parent's sensitivity and becomes hypersensitive to the happiness, not only of themselves, but also of their parent. This can develop an unhealthy co-dependent, enmeshed relationship, where boundaries are blurred and a dependency is developed for both child and parent.

However, parents who take a punitive parental approach are missing the opportunity to teach their child adaptive skills to address their anxiety. Addressing your child's anxious behavior as a discipline problem is missing the boat completely. Yes, it may seem effective in the short run, but that is not for the reasons one might think. Children become intimidated and fearful of the authoritarian parent. Anxious children typically like to please others and they strive to be "good" for their strict parent. There are fewer tantrums, meltdowns and battles for control, but what does the toddler learn? The toddler learns to internalize their feelings but never learns how to problem solve or express their feelings.

Two very different parenting styles, on the opposite sides of the spectrum, create the same results—toddlers who never develop problem-solving skills or the ability to self-regulate. Children can thrive with many different types of parenting approaches, including the two described above. Unfortunately, that is not necessarily true with anxious children. Anxious toddlers, along with toddlers in general, are building their foundational understanding of the world around them. They are building their roadmap for how they will navigate their environment moving forward. Anxious toddlers come into this world with misperceptions, hypersensitivities and mood instability. As parents you have a choice to either teach them an alternative view of their environment or reconfirm the fears they have of the world around them.

Anxious toddlers do best with a parent who "anchors" them. Think of the anxious toddler as an unanchored boat and the rough waves as their anxiety. Without an anchor, your child will be at the whim of the waves. Children do not need a companion in their boat, they need a parent to be the anchor that stabilizes the boat. You have to ask yourself, "Do I jump into the boat to hold my child? Do I get so angry I create more rough waves that my child must navigate through? Or do I unemotionally provide the anchor in their storm?" This can be challenging for any parent! I call it "robotic parenting" and it is a skill that most of us can master no more than probably half the time. You are human, and emotions will get the better of you at times, but aiming to be devoid of intense emotion when parenting is a goal to strive towards.

Teaching, processing feelings, redirecting and disciplining without emotion can be very effective and productive for the anxious child. Without the parent's emotional response, toddlers are not distracted and are better able to focus on their own behavior. When a parent cries when their child is upset, that child is trying to cope with their feelings, but now layered on top of that are their parent's feelings. When a parent has an intense emotional response it can be reconfirming to the child that everything is not alright. Conversely, the parent who shouts and yells clouds the child's thoughts with confusion, guilt and hurt. If the parent remains calm when disciplining, the parent–child relationship is not part of the equation. The child cannot deflect what is happening and has to confront their emotions head on. This reduces comments like, "Why are you mad at me?" or "Why are you shouting at me?" and lets you deal with the real issue of the meltdown.

Routine

Like most toddlers, the anxious toddler loves routine—who doesn't? The difference between a typical toddler and an anxious toddler is what happens when that routine is broken. Toddlers love the predictability and comfort of knowing what to expect and what is coming next. Even though toddlers like their routines, they can usually adapt when schedules unexpectedly change. Moms on a playdate can skip the nap until later and have a spontaneous lunch out with friends. Their toddler might be crankier and more tired than usual, but everyone survives with little to no drama. Not so with the anxious toddler. Routine is less about comfort and more about necessity for most of these kids.

So should parents live by a strict routine, not messing with the delicate balance of maintaining their child's happy mood? Or should parents force their child to be flexible and have no routine—living moment by moment, day by day? Like most approaches outlined in this book, the answer will be somewhere in the middle.

Parents who live by the clock and give their child the predictability of tight schedules and neatly organized and constructed days are not giving their child the opportunity to learn flexibility and adaption skills. Their child is not given the exposure to or experience of change and unpredictability. Children need to be taught that although routine is comforting and preferable, sometimes life has different plans!

Conversely, those who live by the seat of their pants and have no structure to their days are probably exacerbating their toddler's anxiety. Most toddlers thrive on routine and like to know what is coming next. The anxious toddler will live in a hyper-alert state due to not knowing what the day will bring. If the toddler is always in a hyper-alert state, they are more likely to have frequent meltdowns and power struggles.

The art is finding the balance between predictability and spontaneity in your day. In general, it is helpful to keep some structure to your daily routine. Routines can be centered on how you do activities versus what time and in what order you do them. You can have predictability in your bath-time routine or your bedtime routine, for example, but the order and time of day can be altered depending on what occurs throughout that day. Yes, you may usually have a bath before bedtime, but sometimes it may not be possible and your child has to adapt to a change in the schedule.

When schedules change or unexpected plans emerge, it is helpful for parents not always to try to avoid those changes. Life will provide spontaneity and plans will change with little notice once in a while. Take these changes as a painful gift! These learning moments will happen naturally throughout your parenting. These changes give you an opportunity to explain to your child that things do not always stay the same and that sometimes plans change. Tell your child the new schedule. Let them know what will be happening and outline the new plans. The key to building flexibility is exposure to change. This will take some time and will not happen over night.

Empathize with the child when plans change. Like many issues we'll discuss, it is always best to start with validating your child's feelings. They will feel heard and understood. "You are mad because you wanted to go to the park. I am sad too. I wanted to go and play with you. There are things that happen that we can't control." Let your child know what the rest of the day will look like with the change of plans.

"Previewing" what will be happening the next moment, or the next day for that matter, is a helpful tool when working with your anxious child. This helps the child prepare for what is to come. When plans change, you preview the changes and what they should expect. "We have to go to Grandma's house because Mommy forgot some things over there. We will be there for just a little while—enough time for a snack and then a kiss goodbye. We will then come back home." Young children don't understand the concept of time, so it is better to use activities that give them a sense of time.

Depending on your child's personality, it might be helpful to outline what will be happening the next day. When previewing what will happen throughout the day, try to be as specific as possible. As we saw from Sam's story, young children can get overwhelmed if they are unsure of what to expect. Tell your child details like, "We are going over to Maggie's house. We will play with her toys, have a snack and then go home before dinner. Maggie has a small, happy dog that will try and lick you. He likes to climb on people, but he is very friendly and won't hurt you."

Try not to pre-arrange fewer obstacles for your child unless absolutely necessary. In the short term, calling Maggie and asking her to put her small dog away would avoid a possible meltdown, but allowing your child to be exposed to the challenge will help them in the long run.

Even though an anxious child dreads change, they can drive parents crazy when they are excited about a future event! They might repeatedly ask you when the next holiday or birthday will be occurring. They might grow anxious about not knowing exactly when things will be happening. They might require that you repeatedly tell them over and over again when the day will arrive.

Calendars help young children get a sense of what is coming next. Although toddlers don't have a concept of dates, they do understand basic counting and "sleeps." You can put a calendar on their wall and tell them, "We will go on our trip in three sleeps," and let them mark off the days each night before they go to bed. I would recommend using a countdown only for events your child is excited about.

Songs help transitions and can be used frequently throughout the day. You can have a song when it is time to go, time to take a bath, time to clean up etc. I have had parents make up very simplistic songs that the child can sing along with, such as, "Bath time is fun time! Bath time is fun time! Who wants to take a bath?" These songs can help prepare the child for change and make the transition smoother and more fun.

Rigidity

One of the biggest challenges is the level of rigidity that most anxious children exhibit. These children depend on their routine to such a degree that it can be characterized as more ritualistic than routine oriented. They want certain cups and plates, they want to sit in certain spots, they want you to say phrases in certain ways and soon. Helping your child through this is like balancing on a tightrope. You want to help your child adjust to change and yet you do not want to create an acute state of panic within them. This will require you to learn your child's emotional cues and respond accordingly.

Children give off distress cues. These cues can start off as subtle and move into the not so subtle! It is important to zero in on the non-verbal signs your child exhibits when distressed. Your ability to read your child's distress cues will be helpful as you try the approaches outlined in this book. Many methods in this book will require you to judge how emotionally distressed your child is becoming in order to know when to push forward and when to pull back. When you gauge that your child is doing okay, you can continue to help them challenge their fears and rigidity.

Distress cues can vary from child to child. Some distress cues are universal to all toddlers and some cues are unique to a particular child. As you observe your child getting distressed, you might start picking up on their cues. Some examples of common distress cues include, but are not limited to:

> biting or sucking on lower lip
> biting nails
> twirling hair
> looking down
> mumbling or talking without their mouth moving
> growling or whining
> clutching onto your leg
> looking for or holding their transitional object (blanket or stuffed animal)
> regressive talk (baby talk)
> regressive behavior (crawling around)

> refusing to talk or make eye contact
> sitting in a corner or hiding under furniture
> increase in hyperactivity
> pulling at their clothes
> pushing and throwing toys
> stuttering or stammering their words
> asking the same question repeatedly
> peeing or pooping in their pants (when they are already potty trained).

When you and your child are both in a good emotional place and you are not seeing any distress cues, you might take that opportunity to alter your child's ritualistic behavior. This might mean giving your child a different cup or having them sit in a different seat. It might mean cutting their food into triangles instead of squares one day. These are what I call "challenges." Challenges are purposeful situations set up to challenge your child for hands-on learning and skill building. You can help your child walk through these challenges by saying things like, "Sometimes your food is in squares and sometimes it is in triangles, but it will taste the same" or "The red plate is dirty and it has to be washed. The blue plate is good too, and your food will taste just the same." These challenges might cause meltdowns and may seem more trouble than they are worth, but trust me, they *are* worth it in the long run! The more exposure your child has to these challenges and teaching moments, the quicker they will adapt and become more flexible.

That being said, it is important that you assess your child's emotional state prior to and during a challenge. Obviously, if your child is having a rough day already, this would not be a day to do challenges! If you are having a smooth sailing day and you are feeling up to the challenge yourself, then it is worth trying to do. Once you start a challenge, it is important not to accommodate the child halfway through. That is why it is important to gauge your child's mood (and yours) prior to beginning the challenge.

When you tell your child the blue plate is just as good as the red plate, but then halfway through the challenge you give up and give them the red plate, what message are you sending your child? Maybe the red plate *was* better? Maybe if they scream long enough and loud enough you will give them what they want? The message is that you will eventually fix situations that make them uncomfortable and there is no need for them to adapt.

If your child is becoming emotionally undone during a challenge, you can talk them through it. "You don't have to eat off the blue plate, but the red plate is dirty and can't be used." Help them problem solve with questions like, "What would you like me to do?" This will help facilitate a conversation (depending on your child's verbal skills). Challenge conversations can go something like this:

Child: I want red plate!

Parent: The red plate is dirty. What do you want me to do?

Child: I don't know!

Parent: Do you want to eat from a yucky, dirty plate?

Child: No!

Parent: Then what should you do? Do you want to eat with no plate?

Child: No!

Parent: Do you want the blue plate?

Child: Fine!

Conversations do not always go as smoothly as the one above, but over time these challenges teach children to think about the problem and not to look blindly to their parents to fix them.

It also teaches parents not to swoop in and accommodate the child in order to avoid conflict between them. When a child independently overcomes an obstacle, their adaptive skills are strengthened.

Other challenges will naturally present themselves in life. As in the example above, Sam's father did not intentionally disrupt the order of his trains. These situations can be wonderful (terrible) learning moments, depending on how you play your cards. If Carla and Tom had the energy and patience, it would be a good time to let Sam work through his emotional discomfort without being rescued. The challenge could have gone something like this:

Sam: My trains! Oh no!

Dad: What's wrong?

Sam: You mess up my trains!

Dad: I didn't know you had it a special way. Show me how it was before.

Sam: (crying) You mess up my trains!

Dad: Did I mean to mess them up?

Sam: No.

Dad: What do you want me to do?

Sam: Fix it!

Dad: You put it the way you like it.

This conversation teaches Sam that accidents happen and actions are not always deliberate. It also teaches him to express his feelings instead of having a meltdown. His parents do not fix the problem for him, but walk him through fixing it himself. This teaches him problem-solving skills.

I often coach parents to robotically teach their kids to say, "Oh well." As simplistic as this may sound, young children can get lost in too much verbal processing. When children are upset they are unable to process much of what you are trying to say to them. Keeping your verbal interactions short and succinct can be more effective. If in the above example Sam did not calm down enough to have a conversation, his parents could repeatedly say to him, "It was an accident, say 'oh well' and fix it." Over time, children will start to say "Oh well" on their own when letting go of an issue and will look to parents for praise when they say it.

Repeat after me

Anxious toddlers will often tell parents what to do or how to do something. They can sometimes view parents as an extension of themselves. It is often easier for a parent just to give in to the child's directional commands than to face the battle that will most likely ensue.

Demands like, "You stand there!" "You give me another hug!" and "Carry me!" are just a few examples. These demands can extend beyond the parent–child interaction and into the child's peer interactions. Children can start demanding that peers play in a certain way and may even give another child a script of exactly what they should say when playing make-believe with them. Toddlers want to control their environment and orchestrate what makes them the most comfortable. Unfortunately, the world, along with future teachers and peers, will not accommodate this type of behavior. It is important to teach your child early on that they control themselves, but they do not control other people. Interactions like the one below can be a helpful way of teaching your child this message:

Child: One more hug!

Parent: I already gave you five hugs! It is time to go night night.

Child: I need another hug!

> Parent: Mommy gave you enough hugs. I love you, but it is time for bed.
>
> Child: Give me a hug!
>
> Parent: You don't tell mommy what to do. You only tell yourself what to do.

Parents sometimes have a hard time with demands for more affection because they feel it is cruel to not acquiesce when their child is asking for more love. What some parents don't understand is that it is not about getting more love, but rather an anxious compulsion that cannot get satiated. The child is looking for reassurance through your words and physical contact, but it will never be enough. Ironically, when you give in to the demand for more and more hugs, the child's compulsion for more hugs grows. When you draw clear boundaries, you teach your child to feel secure with limits and you break their compulsive behavior.

Children's rigid behavior around their routine and their environment can be exhausting and time consuming. It is a hard balancing act, but it is important for parents gently to push their child to the outer limits of their comfort zone. Changing the routine, purposely breaking ritualistic behavior and not letting your child control your behavior will all help them develop long-term coping mechanisms and adaptation skills. It is important to remember though that these things will take time, patience and consistency!

• • • • • • • • • •

CHAPTER 2

Meltdowns

Amanda and Jon

At first Amanda and Jon thought their daughter Ashley's meltdowns were normal and assumed that most parents had to suffer through them. Ashley was their first child and they had read how the "terrible twos" came neatly packaged with screams, stubbornness and stomping feet. However, Amanda started to think that Ashley's behavior may not be as typical as she had initially thought. She realized with shock and embarrassment that she was the only parent consistently carrying her child, kicking and screaming, at the end of each playdate or visit to the park.

Amanda felt as if her life had turned into surviving one tantrum at a time. She was constantly on edge and worried about when the next tantrum would catch her off guard, throwing her day and her routine completely off schedule. Amanda and Jon knew telling Ashley "No" would guarantee a 10–15-minute tantrum, but there were other times when they had no idea what would set her off. Well-intentioned friends and family would tell Amanda that Ashley was just a little "spoiled" and that she just needed to be more firmly disciplined. This was especially insulting to Amanda, who worked so hard at being a good parent.

Although it was a nice reprieve when Ashley took a nap during the day, her meltdowns on waking were confusing and upsetting.

• • • • • •

Often after her naps, Ashley would cry until she was sweaty and exhausted. Despite their efforts to calm her, Ashley was often inconsolable for 15–30 minutes and they had no idea why.

Sometimes Ashley's demands were irrational or unreasonable. She went through a phase where she would ask for chocolate milk, but when Amanda poured the milk she would scream, "No! I just want chocolate!" Despite her mom's efforts to explain that you need milk for chocolate milk, Ashley would just ball up on the floor and scream whenever she saw her mom pour the white milk into her cup. Amanda found herself sneaking into the pantry to pour the "banned" milk before she added the toddler-approved chocolate.

Another irrational struggle was over the temperature of food. When Ashley's food was too hot, Amanda would put her bowl in the freezer to cool down. Ashley would become frantically upset when her food disappeared into the freezer. Amanda would get frustrated and give Ashley her hot food back. To Amanda's dismay, Ashley would get equally upset when she got her bowl back and her food was still too hot. Ashley would throw the bowl off the table. Amanda and Jon were at a loss as to what to do. It seemed like no matter what they tried to do, Ashley would find a reason still to be upset.

Jon felt bad that he didn't enjoy going to the park with Ashley. Amanda worked sometimes at the weekend and Jon and Ashley were on their own some days. Jon hated to admit it, but he was nervous to take Ashley out in public. What if she had a meltdown? What if he couldn't control her? He had started taking her to the park near their block. He thought—how bad can this get? Unfortunately, the answer was, pretty bad!

Jon naively thought things were going well the first time he took Ashley to the park. After an hour, Jon was feeling pretty good about the whole outing and told Ashley it was time to go. Like a dormant volcano starting to come to life, Ashley's happy face started to turn red with rage, "Noooo! I play more!" Despite Jon's efforts to reason with her, Ashley grew increasingly upset. The whole situation got progressively more out of control until

Jon was forced to pick Ashley up and carry her home kicking and screaming.

Another difficult time for Ashley was around bedtime. Almost like clockwork, as soon as it was time to get her pajamas on, Ashley would have a complete meltdown. She would start running around screaming, "I no tired! I no go to bed!" Her parents would eventually tire of making repeated demands for her to come over and put on her pajamas. Eventually a chase would ensue and once Ashley was inevitably caught, the flailing of arms and legs would begin in full force. The fight to get her little arms and legs into her pajamas was tiring and by the time her teeth were brushed and she was ready for a story, Amanda and Jon were ready for sleep themselves!

Ashley

Ashley often felt as if things did not go her way. She was frequently told "No" and that made her upset. She showed her parents how upset she was by screaming, kicking and falling to the floor. Sometimes they would understand how frustrated she was and they would say "Fine, you can have it—just be quiet!" She happily complied.

When Ashley woke up from a nap her head felt weird and she felt out of it. She didn't like the way she felt and it scared her. Why did everything seem so fuzzy? She would scream in panic. She would get further confused when her parents seemed frustrated by her complete panic and meltdown. Why weren't they helping her feel less fuzzy and out of it?! This made her mad and she would scream even harder!

Often Ashley's parents would frustrate her because they did not seem to get what she was saying at all! She did not like the taste of white milk and preferred chocolate milk. She clearly asked her mom for chocolate milk and she just ignored her request and started pouring white milk into her cup! Why wasn't she listening to her! She would scream, "No, just chocolate!" over and over again, but her mom kept arguing with her.

Once Ashley was so hungry! She couldn't wait to eat her mac-n-cheese. She had waited for what seemed like forever until her mom finally put the bowl in front of her. Yummy! She got a big spoonful and tried to negotiate it steadily to her open mouth. She was so excited the spoon was making it all the way to her lips when suddenly—OUCH! It burned her mouth! She started to cry and her mom quickly took her food away from her and put it in the freezer! Why was her mom putting her food away? She was so hungry! She started to scream, "I hungry! Give it back!" Her mom seemed annoyed. Shouldn't she have been the one who was annoyed? She was the starving one! Finally her mom got the idea and gave her the bowl back from the freezer. She excitedly maneuvered the spoon close to her mouth again but then a now-familiar sensation of burning enveloped her lips. Not again! She screamed and threw the bowl off the table! "I give up," she thought!

Ashley loved to go to the park. When it was just her and her dad she would get so bored at home. One day he had announced that he was taking her to the park. She was so excited! Finally they were going to have some fun! At the park she ran through the playground equipment with excitement and curiosity. The last time she had been to the park she had been too scared to go down the slide. She had felt that she could be braver and she had been right! She slid down the slide with trepidation initially, but eventually with complete disregard. She had finally mastered the slide when she had heard her dad call her. "No!" she thought. "We can't leave now! I just mastered the slide." She had been engulfed in her slide challenge and had not been prepared to leave! She screamed and tried to run away from her dad. She had thought maybe he would give up, but that was not how the park visit ended.

Nighttime was a scary time for Ashley. She hated it when it started to get dark because that meant dark rooms, scary shadows and being alone. Sometimes it would get dark, but bedtime didn't come for a long time. Other times it would get dark and it was bedtime soon after. One thing was for sure, once *her pajamas were on, bedtime was sure to follow! She thought that if she could stop her parents from getting her pajamas on, she'd never have to face the torture of bedtime. She would run around the room for dear life! When they caught her, she'd scream as if her life depended on it—because frankly, that's how she felt.*

Accepting no

Most toddlers have meltdowns when they do not get their way. In fact, you can say that this is probably at the root of most toddler tantrums. Toddlers are just finding their independence and are ready to take charge—if only you weren't standing in their way! They know best and get very, *very* upset when you think that is not true.

Like all toddlers, anxious toddlers have meltdowns when told "No" as well. The only difference is that anxious toddlers have a hard time regulating most things, including their emotions. So, when an anxious toddler starts to derail because they can't get their way, their tantrums are going to be longer and more intense than those of the average toddler.

I look at the toddler phase as the time to lay down the foundation for their future development and success. Imagine you are building a house. The ground is soft and unstable and it is important to lay down the foundation to build a solid structure on top of it. Laying the foundation is not the most glamorous or exciting part of building a house, but if it is not done right, the structure is not sound and everything built on top of it can crumble.

Most of what you teach your toddler is foundational building. It will often feel as if your efforts are not effective, but in fact you are laying out the ground work on which everything else will be built. When parents tell me, "We didn't worry about the behavior—he was just two" or "We gave in when he was little, after all he was just a toddler," I think they have not realized the significance of pouring the concrete into the early stages of development.

In reality, you are giving your young child a blueprint of how to view limits and boundaries. You are teaching your child whether your words have meaning or whether they are empty words without value. You are letting your child know, by your actions, if their tantrums have power. If you reinforce negative behavior, it will persevere. If you reinforce positive behavior, it will persevere—it is as simple as that. Your child takes your lead and paints their reality based on what you teach them about the world they live in. If you teach them that "No" can turn to "Yes" and that screaming and kicking leads to them getting what they want, they will have those expectations for everyone who interacts with them, including teachers and peers.

In order to understand how you parent, you may have to look at your marriage or further back to your own childhood. I have had many parents tell me that they are "making up" for their strict spouse. I have been told by despondent parents, "Sometimes my spouse is just so strict, I feel bad for the kids and I feel like I need to overcompensate." Parents will say "Yes" when their spouse says "No" because they empathize with their child and then parent out of guilt. Most parents I have worked with realize this flaw in their parenting, but have a hard time changing their behavior. Usually, until they feel more comfortable with how their spouse parents their child, this pattern will not change.

Sometimes your childhood can shape your parenting style. I have worked with parents who have told me, "My parents were so abusive, I don't want to be anything like that with my kids!" Unfortunately, this way of thinking can paralyze parents and cause them to struggle with setting healthy boundaries or limits for their children. Conversely, I have had other parents tell me, "When my dad wasn't looking, my mom would always give me what I wanted. She just told me not to tell my dad."

Parents who enjoyed that type of childhood tend to emulate that parenting style with their own kids. Some parents think this behavior exemplifies their love for their child. They may also have the misguided belief that when they are in cahoots with their child, it makes their bond even closer. Unfortunately, this bond is at the expense of the relationship with the other parent. They will say things like, "I guess I spoil him. I just can't say no to him." What these parents don't always realize is that they are doing a disservice to their spouse *and* their child. Their child is not learning to take boundaries or rules seriously and they are learning that one parent's parental control is a facade. This undermines the other parent and teaches the child that their parents are not a united front. This is unfair to the spouse who is typically unaware that such divisiveness is occurring in their family dynamics.

Another potential barrier to successful parenting is the parent's own anxiety. It is not surprising that a large percentage of toddlers who have anxiety have parents who suffer from anxiety. Given the genetic component to anxiety in general, this is to be expected. The positive aspect of having anxiety yourself is that you can relate to and understand your child's behavior on a deeper level. The negative aspect is that some anxious parents get overwhelmed by their child's anxiety and have a hard time coping with the stress of having an anxious toddler. I have worked with parents who cry along with their child when their child doesn't want to go to school. I have met parents who need to sleep with their child as much as their child needs to sleep with them. These parents will express fear for their child's safety and feel a great deal of comfort knowing that their child is right next them as they sleep. These parents also struggle with their child's strong negative emotions. Their child's inability to self-regulate triggers a sense of doom and anxiety within themselves. Driven to fix this unsettling feeling, anxious parents may opt to quickly "fix" the situation for their child and in so doing, reduce the anxiety level of both their child and themselves. I often hear parents say, "I just felt so bad. He looked so sad, so I just gave him what he wanted."

One of the hardest challenges for toddlers is accepting the word "No." It is your job as a parent to teach your toddler that, unfortunately, they will not always get everything they want. Although it is tiring and exhausting to hear your child scream and scream, it is a valuable lesson you are teaching them. Toddlers are going to scream and be upset at times. They cannot move on and develop other methods of self-regulating until they know for sure that their screaming and kicking won't change the situation. Over time your toddler will start to see that their tantrums do not pay off and they will learn to let go sooner.

At the beginning of a tantrum, a toddler may feel that you do not fully understand what they want. Part of the tantrum is built on frustration. Toddlers may think, "If she knew what I wanted, she'd give it to me!" So, the first step in helping your child with a tantrum is to let them know you understand why they are mad. A conversation might go like this:

Child: I want that toy!

Parent: That's his toy, not yours.

Child: Give me toy! (Child starts to cry)

Parent: You are mad because you want his toy.

Child: Yes!

Parent: But, you can't have his toy because it is not yours.

Child: Noooo! I want it!

Parent: I know and that makes you mad.

This conversation will not eliminate the ensuing tantrum, but it helps the child understand that you know what they want, but are still not giving in. It is also helpful to start labeling your child's feelings. Not only does this make the child feel understood, it helps them build an emotional vocabulary that they can start using in the future. As your toddler gets a little older, they might even correct you when you are labeling their feelings with a more accurate word to describe how they feel, such as, "I not sad… I'm mad!" This will show you that your child is starting to grow their emotional vocabulary.

Toddlers like to throw tantrums and no matter how wonderful a parent you are, your child is going to have moments where they cannot accept no. When your child goes into their full-fledged meltdown, the best response is no response. No matter how intelligent your child is, they lose all ability to reason or understand you when they are in a full-blown meltdown. They also lose the skills of good communication. This means that essentially all understanding and communication shuts down when your toddler starts to have a meltdown.

Once a child is having a full-blown tantrum, the only job for the parent is to keep the child safe and contained. Parents will often ask how they can stop a tantrum, but once it has begun it is too late. Putting a child in time out for having a tantrum does not help them learn how to self-regulate and may teach them that expressing their feelings is not allowed. Having a "robotic," repetitive response to your child will help them move on quicker. Making comments like, "No means no" periodically helps your child realize that their tantrum is having no effect on the outcome of the situation. If your child continues to scream and they are disturbing those around them, you can say, "You are hurting our ears. If you want to keep crying, go into the other room." If your child screams, "No, I don't want to go!" then you can respond with, "If you stay here you must stop crying." This allows your child to make their own choice and encourages quicker self-regulation. If your child refuses to leave the room, but continues to cry, tell them if they do not stop crying you will pick them up and place them in a quiet room. Having said this, no parental approach to toddler tantrums will be fully effective—sorry! This is one of those developmental phases that has to run its course. As parents, all you can do is help your toddler develop skills to eventually self-regulate.

Meltdowns after naps

Now that we have covered the common reasons why toddlers have tantrums, we will address tantrums that are more common in anxious toddlers. Although typical toddlers may be cranky when they wake up from a nap, anxious toddlers can have prolonged meltdowns on awakening. These unprovoked meltdowns are confusing for parents. As mentioned earlier, anxious toddlers have difficulty self-regulating in all areas of their life. This includes their mood and their sleep cycles. Anxious toddlers tend to be hypersensitive to subtle changes both internally (e.g. temperature) and externally (e.g. noises). These sensitivities make it hard for children to move from a sleep state to an alert state. When they wake up prematurely or they go from a deep sleep to an alert state, they have a physiological response that makes them feel unsettled and disoriented. Toddlers don't know how to handle this change other than to have a meltdown.

Unfortunately there is not much you can do about this tantrum. Parents will desperately ask their child, "What is wrong?!" only to be met with an escalating scream. Further efforts to calm your child ("Do you want a drink?" "Do you want to watch TV?") will be met with an increase in anger and hostility.

The best way to handle the situation is to limit your verbal interaction with your child. Distract your child by putting on the television. They need a passive activity that can take their attention away from how they are feeling. This can often reduce the length of the tantrum. Put water or food next to them—

sometimes food or drink can help make them feel better. Some children like to be gently, rhythmically tapped. Other children do not like to be touched at all during these times, so touch at your own risk! These tantrums are more likely to happen if your child's sleep is interrupted. If you see your child wake up, wait for them to come to fully before approaching them or greeting them. Some children need to get to a completely alert state before they can interact with others and sometimes they might stir and then fall back to sleep. Giving your child space as they wake up will help them reach that level of alertness without them feeling overwhelmed.

Irrational behavior

Anxious toddlers have a hard time accepting the obvious. They get upset about things that the parent cannot control. These tantrums tend to be more frustrating because they seem so ridiculous and irrational. When your toddler is screaming at the top of their lungs, "I want apple sauce!" and you are all out of apple sauce, what are you supposed to do? You do the obvious thing and show your child that there is no apple sauce anywhere to be found, but they still continue to scream! This may be the part where you lose your cool and start to have a tantrum yourself!

When children are being irrational, it is better to get them to realize the problem on their own. They may still be upset, but you begin to teach them problem-solving and critical-thinking skills. The conversation might go something like this:

Child: I want apple sauce!

Parent: We are all out of apple sauce.

Child: Give me apple sauce!

Parent: (Opens refrigerator and holds toddler up) Do you see any?

Child: No.

Parent: Where do you want me to get some?

Child: I don't know.

The conversation will probably go round in circles like this for quite a while, but you are allowing your child to assess the situation and come to the same conclusion on their own. Like many of the approaches in this book, it won't necessarily stop the behavior immediately, but you are starting to foster independent thinking and problem-solving skills.

Another approach for minor upsets, especially those that don't make much sense, is distraction. This is a powerful tool in the battle of toddler mood swings. A toddler's attention can often be quickly redirected. If your child is just starting to get upset, redirect their focus to something else.

Child: I want to sit on your lap.

Parent: No, I am writing something.

Child: I want to sit on your LAP!

Parent: What's your baby doll doing? Is she hungry?

Child: (Gets up to find her baby doll)

Even if the distraction doesn't last forever, it is a nice reprieve from the battle. If the issue was minor, distraction is usually enough to permanently refocus the child. Distraction may not always work, but it is a nice tool to have in your parental toolbox.

Transitions

Transitions are one of a toddler's least favorite experiences. In general, toddlers do not like change, but this dislike for change is magnified for the anxious toddler. Moving from one activity to another can provoke trepidation, fear and especially stubbornness. Children are just learning to exert their independence and they get very upset and unbudging when you tell them to move on to the next thing or activity. Sometimes this unwillingness to move on can turn into an all-out war!

It's important for parents to realize that a transition can be something as simple as moving from lunchtime to nap time or bath time to bedtime. Any changes in activity require your toddler to adapt, switch gears and refocus on the new task at hand. We move through our day rapidly changing activities without much thought or concern. We wonder why toddlers can't do that as well. Why is it so hard to go from brushing your teeth to hopping into the bath?

The mind of a toddler is a complex and tricky thing to navigate. They do not have a sense of time and they often do not have an understanding of what is coming next. Toddlers live in the moment and even though they may know that nap time comes after lunchtime, they do not always have the ability always to look at the big picture. They tend to get engrossed in most of their activities and are shocked when it is time to move on!

As we discussed in Chapter 1, previewing can help reduce your toddler's emotional distress about transitions. It is a key tool when helping your anxious toddler and worth exploring further as we talk about transitions. When you "preview" you are letting your child know what is coming next. You can preview the week, the day or the afternoon. It is helpful to keep your child informed of what is coming ahead. This helps reduce your child's anxiety and lets them prepare for changes.

Previewing the next day or week is helpful for some toddlers and anxiety-producing for others. Some children perseverate over every activity and get overwhelmed by future plans. You can tell if your child is like this if they seem unsettled after you preview what is coming up next. If they are uncomfortable or anxious, they may ask repetitive questions about what will be happening. If your child is typically nervous about future plans, it is best not to preview too far in advance and just stick to previewing a few hours into the future.

Previewing might generally be an effective tool for your child, but if a particularly stressful event is coming up you may not want to preview it until a few hours before it is about to happen. This may be true for events like doctor's appointments. Conversely, a particularly fun event might bring about too much stimulation and excitement. If you don't want to hear questions like, "Are we going today?" and "Is it time to go to the party yet?" it is best to preview these types of activities closer to the event or your child will drive you crazy!

Naming your days might help the effectiveness of your previewing. If your child has different caregivers or different classes on various days you can name those days (e.g. "Mommy day" "swim class day" and "Sunday family day"). When you name your days, your child will immediately have an understanding of what happens on that day. For instance, when you tell your child it is "swim class day" they know that means Mommy is home with them and they go to swim class. When you tell them it is a "family day" they already know that their whole family will be at home, they will not have to drop anyone off at school and the family will go on a bike ride together. Previewing at bedtime can be helpful for many anxious children. It might go something like this:

> Tomorrow is a Mommy day. We are going to wake up and take your brother to school. We are going to play at home and then we are going to pick your brother up from school. Daddy will come home and we will all have dinner together and then it will be time for bath and bed.

Some children may not need this much detail and it might suffice to just say, "Tomorrow is a Mommy day."

Toddlers have selective memories. They may remember the smallest detail about a trip that happened a year ago, but they can forget what you are doing tomorrow—even after you have told them repeatedly. Therefore, previewing does not happen once, but is an ongoing approach. You preview the next day at bedtime and when you wake up you preview what is going to happen for the next few hours. Even if your child does not seem to care if you preview their day, it can be a beneficial tool in eliminating transitional meltdowns.

Warnings are another key tool in the transitional battle. This may not eradicate your toddler's refusal to move on when an activity is over, but it will ideally lessen the intensity. You cannot give enough warnings prior to the end of an activity! In a perfect world it is best to avoid time-based warnings such as, "In ten minutes we are leaving." Ten minutes—what does that mean? Preferably try to anchor time in activities, saying such things as, "You can go down the slide two more times and then we are going to leave," or "After we eat the cake we are going to be leaving the party." This gives your child a much more concrete understanding of when the activity will end.

Realistically you will sometimes use time as a warning. When it is not possible to give activity-based indicators that the event is over, you can use time in a way that your child will learn its meaning. You can use the countdown of ten, five, and three minutes. Your child will have no concept of what you are saying, but they will learn that when you say ten they still have some time to play, but when you say three their time is almost up. Do not alter how many minutes you use. If you always stick to the ten, five and three minutes, you will help the concept solidify in your child's mind.

When it is time to go, have your child stop playing and engage them in another activity such as cleaning up or getting their shoes on. You want to try and help your child disengage from their current activity before they have to think about leaving the event. If they are completely engrossed in an activity and then you abruptly tell them it is time to go, you are guaranteed a transitional meltdown. For instance, if your child is on a playdate you might tell them, "It's time to start cleaning up," and this helps them disengage from their current activity. If they are fully disengaged from the activity they were engrossed in, hearing "We are leaving" will not be as difficult for them.

When your child is having a hard time leaving, it can be beneficial to redirect their attention to what they will be doing next. Even if there is nothing exciting happening on the horizon, you can be creative with your wording, such as, "We are going to go home and cook dinner. Do you want to help me cook? I love it when you are my helper!" Getting your child excited about the next activity helps reduce the resistance you'll get when leaving the previous activity.

Sometimes anxious children have a hard time leaving something incomplete. This happens when they are in the middle of an art project or are busy coming down a slide. It is important to observe your child's activities long before you are going to leave. If you see your child is in the middle of something that they won't be able to finish before you leave, you can help them complete it. Anxious toddlers will have a total meltdown if they are not able to finish an activity they are working on. You are asking for a nasty fight if you stop their activity before they are finished—and frankly it's not worth it! If you see them starting a new activity that they will not be able to complete in the time you have left, it is best to not let them start the new project. If your child is not already fully immersed in an activity, it is easier to get them to move on.

Overstimulated, tired explosions

When toddlers are tired, they are cranky! When toddlers are cranky, they tend to have more tantrums! As we have discussed, anxious toddlers are more sensitive to internal changes in their body. They have a harder time coping with feelings of exhaustion and are therefore prone to even more tantrums than your typical toddler.

Tired tantrums are hard to avoid. When trying to discover the origin of why your child is having frequent meltdowns the first question should be—are they tired?

If the answer is yes, there is no point in trying to address the minor infraction that has caused them to meltdown in the first place. It is better to help the child realize that they are getting upset because they are tired. Tell your child, "You are grumpy because you are tired." The child will most likely scream back, "No I am NOT!" Despite your child's refusal, it is helpful to give your child a name for what they are feeling. As discussed earlier, labeling various feelings will help your child develop a vocabulary to match their emotions. Growing their emotional vocabulary will help move your toddler from the non-verbal tantrum to them verbally expressing their feelings.

Many toddlers don't want to admit that they still need a nap. Some will refuse a nap even when they are rubbing their little red raccoon eyes. If your toddler is not a napper, but they are acting cranky, try to get them involved in a sedentary activity. If they are lying on the couch watching TV, you can rub their head or pat their back to get them to slow down and this may reduce further irritability.

I do it myself! You do it for me!

Although toddlers may seem like a homogenous group of cuteness and frustration, they are all uniquely different. The one thing you can count on, however, is that they tend to be one extreme or the other. Toddlers are either fiercely independent or want everything done for them. Either behavior can cause tantrums on a daily basis.

The fiercely independent "little person" demands that they do it themselves, but sadly they often do not have the capability of doing so. They want to put on their own clothes, their own socks and their own shoes! Frustrated parents sit back in annoyance and horror as their little child contorts, grimaces and wiggles their way out of their shirt. It is not a sight for the faint hearted, but dare to interrupt the process and you will get an enraged toddler who will scream, "I do it myself!"

This personality trait is actually—dare I say—a strength. Yes, this is a positive attribute! Children who show a willingness to persevere and work through their challenges will most likely have the same stick-with-it attitude throughout life's challenges. So, sit back, take a patience pill and do not interrupt the process of ugly independence. This can be very difficult to do, especially if your toddler is getting more and more frustrated and you've seen them pass the arm hole five times! The worst thing to do is to touch the "little person" without their permission. This will send them into a full throttle meltdown that can most likely be avoided. Do not approach without permission. Throw out a simple, "Can I help?" and, depending on your child's personality, you will get a "Yes" or an adamant "No!" If you are not allowed to offer a hand, a verbal direction might be needed, such as, "That's an arm hole—it's not for your head."

On the flip side, there are toddlers who would like to stay young forever and do not like the idea of growing up. They want their parent to do everything for them. This can be especially tricky if you are a parent who doesn't want your child to grow up either. Even though it is faster and might even feel more rewarding to do things for our children, it is not fostering their healthy independence. If you continue to do things for your child, inadvertently you are giving them the message that they are not capable of doing it themselves. Failure is part of success and if we take that part of the equation out of our children's lives, we are stripping them of good life skills.

For the reluctant, dependent toddler, you can start with simple, small steps. If they refuse to get their own underwear on you can hold their underwear while they negotiate their little legs into each hole. As they master each step, you can do less and less for them. Your refusal to do an entire task for them will inevitably cause a meltdown. These meltdowns are worth it, because discovering their own capabilities and the ability to fight through challenges is a lesson you don't want them to miss.

Anxiety meltdowns

One meltdown that is unique to the anxious toddler is the anxiety meltdown. This can be confusing to parents because if you are not in tune with your child's anxiety you might misconstrue the reason for the meltdown. Unfortunately, the meltdown itself looks like any other run-of-the-mill toddler meltdown, the difference is the context and situation in which it occurs.

Toddlers do not have a large enough vocabulary to convey effectively what is bothering them. When they are feeling overwhelmed or scared, one common response is to shut down or to throw a tantrum. If your child is having a tantrum around the same time each night, it is wise to look for patterns. To find patterns, look at what is happening directly before a tantrum or what is supposed to be happening around the time of a tantrum. Are they going to have a playdate? Are you leaving them with a babysitter? Is it almost mealtime?

Bedtime is a common reason for an anxiety meltdown. Many parents have told me, "He's fine, he is just avoiding going to bed." The deeper question is—why is he avoiding going to bed? Is the reason as simple as "He wants to play more" or is it possibly that he is afraid of bedtime? If your toddler wants you to lie down with them or they can't fall asleep unless you are next to them, they might have some anxiety around sleep. If this is the case, you don't want to fixate on why they won't let you brush their teeth, but rather focus on the true issue—how to make them feel safer at bedtime. I cover bedtime struggles and approaches in detail in Chapter 4.

When you think the meltdown is caused by fear, label your child's feelings for them. You can say, "You don't like bedtime, do you? Bedtime scares you, huh?" This helps your child feel understood and allows you to get to the heart of the matter. If you are wrong, your child might correct you or disagree with you—this is helpful too!

You might see anxiety-triggered meltdowns in various situations your child encounters. They might be more irritated or moody prior to going to pre-school or daycare. They might have more frequent meltdowns before a class that instills some nervousness, such as a swim class or a music class. Your child might have meltdowns before a birthday party or before having a large number of people over. It is important to look at the bigger picture when your anxious toddler is having a meltdown, and to avoid getting caught up in the minor battle that may be happening in front of you!

• • • • • • • • • • • • • • • • • •

CHAPTER 3

Mealtime Struggles

Susan and Richard

Susan and Richard dreaded dinner time. In the past, this was the time of day they loved the most. They would sit at the table with their two children and would catch up on everyone's day. Dinner was a bonding time for their family—a time they got to reconnect and all be together. Since they had their third child, dinner had never been the same. As a baby, Kate would often have a hard time breastfeeding and Susan would have to leave the table to breastfeed her in a quiet room. Kate had acid reflux and would often cry in pain after she ate.

Susan and Richard thought that once they transferred Kate to solid foods, life would get back to normal, but that was not the case. Kate had a hard time moving to solid foods and would gag on any food that had mixed textures. Yogurt with fruit and cottage cheese would make Kate throw up. Her parents were baffled. Why would Kate throw up sometimes when she ate? She seemed to do better with crackers, pasta and cereals. Soon they found themselves only giving Kate a handful of foods each day. They worried about her health and were concerned about whether she was getting enough nutritional sustenance. Their pediatrician assured them that she would not "starve herself to death," but she wasn't putting on much weight.

Kate's behavior around food became more and more difficult. She didn't like to sit at the table and would often have a tantrum and refuse to eat when the family sat down for dinner. She would throw food from the tray and would try to wiggle out of her highchair. She took all of her parents' energy and they were not able to focus their attention on their other two children. Richard and Susan felt guilty that Kate took so much of their time away.

Kate didn't like to get her hands dirty and when she ate something messy, she'd often become distraught when she couldn't get her hands clean. Midway through a meal, Kate would scream, "Hands dirty! Wash them! Wash them!" and the meal would be interrupted in order to clean Kate's hands. Once Kate's hands were clean, she would refuse to keep eating the food that made her messy in the first place.

Sometimes when Kate was eating, she would open up her mouth and let all the food tumble out. He mom would yell at her and tell her to not spit her food out, but Kate wouldn't listen. Two bites later, Kate would be spitting food out of her mouth again. Susan tried giving her a time out every time she did this, but Kate never seemed to learn. Susan wondered why none of her other children had this problem.

Richard believed Kate was just stubborn and thought they gave in too much. He thought maybe it was because Kate was the baby of the house and got what she wanted. He was worried that Kate was going to teach their other two children that they didn't have to eat what they were served. He didn't want Kate undermining the good eating habits they had instilled in their other two children. He decided to not allow Kate out of her highchair until she ate some of her vegetables. Kate sat screaming in her highchair for over an hour after everyone cleared the table. Her father sat with her and told her she wasn't leaving the table until she ate some of her vegetables. Eventually Kate took a bite of a green bean, but then proceeded to throw it up. Richard decided at that point the battle wasn't worth it! He felt Kate had won once again! From that day on Kate would throw a tantrum the minute she saw vegetables, even when they weren't put directly on her plate.

Susan had the most success when she fed Kate casually throughout the day. She would eat cereal in the morning while watching TV, usually without any issues. She would eat snacks at her little table in between meals without a fuss. Dinner time was by far the worst meal of her day. Eventually, Richard and Susan decided it wasn't worth the disruption to have her eat with them at dinner time, so they fed her an hour earlier and she played in another room while everyone else ate.

Kate

When Kate was a baby she would be enveloped by the warmth and comfort of her mother's breastmilk, only to be abruptly startled out of her relaxed state by a burning feeling coming up from her throat to her mouth. Kate hadn't experienced much pain in her young life and she started to become hyper-alert to when she'd feel the pain again. She started to recognize a pattern— every time she drank milk, she felt pain. Kate started to feel anxious when she breastfed, and other noises and distractions overwhelmed her as she ate. Eventually, her mom took her into a quiet room to breastfeed and she felt more relaxed.

Kate's first year of life was filled with acid-burning pain after she ate. Her stomach always seemed to hurt. Kate grew more and more nervous around eating. It took a while for Kate's parents to realize that she was in pain after she ate. She didn't have the words to tell them that she was in pain and her irritability was hard to decode. Once they realized she had reflux she was put on medication. Eventually, as she got a little bit older the pain stopped, but the knee-jerk reaction to be nervous around eating remained.

Kate had a very sensitive gag reflex and when her tongue suddenly encountered something bumpy or lumpy in something otherwise smooth she would gag or throw up. She became distrusting about what her mom and dad wanted to feed her. What was in it? Would it make her gag or feel like throwing up?

Some food her parents fed her didn't disappear in her mouth. When she ate crackers or dry cereal she would suck and chew on the food and eventually her mouth would be empty. When they gave her something chewy—like meat—she could never get the food to disappear and no matter how long she chewed or sucked on the food, some of it always remained. Kate didn't know what to do with the food that remained in her mouth and it scared her to think about swallowing it. She started to remember which foods wouldn't "disappear" and would refuse to eat them!

There were times when she put too much food in her mouth and she felt overwhelmed. She would put a big fistful of cereal into her mouth and be surprised by how much food she had to make "disappear." She'd get scared that she couldn't handle all that food and she'd let some of it dribble out of her mouth. For some reason her mom didn't like her doing this and would make her sit in time out. This was confusing because she was just trying to eat.

Not only was Kate's mouth sensitive, but so were her hands. She hated to feel a sticky, gloppy mess on her hands. Sometimes even just feeling those types of textures on her hands would make her gag. When she was given messy food, she'd try to eat it without getting dirty, but that was an impossible feat for a toddler! She hadn't mastered a spoon or a fork and often half the food would get all over her tray, hands and face. When her food was splattered all around her, she became anxious and overwhelmed. She was unable to focus on her eating and needed to have her hands cleaned right away.

All of these feeding issues culminated in a state of panic when she was forced to sit in the highchair. The highchair was where all of these struggles happened and her heart would start racing as soon as it was time to eat. She especially didn't like dinner time. Her whole family sat at the table and she was often reprimanded more at that meal than any other meal. She was also fed more mysterious foods at dinner. Often there would be a scary pile of food on her plate that she could not make out. She would see pieces of meat and vegetable and sauce all mixed together and presented in a small heap. Smells and flavors were more exotic at dinner and often there were things she had never before seen. She thought it was best to just avoid the whole thing! She would wiggle and scream and try to get down from her highchair. She would shout, "I not hungry!" but with little success.

One time she wasn't allowed to get out of her highchair until she ate one of the green things. She was pretty sure she had tried one of those things before and did not like it! It didn't smell good and there was no way she was going to put it in her mouth! She screamed and cried, but her dad would not budge. She felt as if she had been at the table forever. Her sister and brother were allowed to leave and she had no idea where her mom went. She thought she might never be allowed to go! Finally she caved in and reluctantly put a green thing in her mouth. Instantly the taste disgusted her. She was trying to chew it when the green bean broke apart in her mouth and different bumpy textures were detected by her tongue. She instantly started to gag and before she knew it she threw up. She promised herself that she would never ever try that again! From then on every time she saw a green thing she panicked and would throw a fit. She grew even more cautious about trying new things.

Eating during the day was much more relaxing. She was given food that was predictable and comforting to her. She thought she could eat cereal, crackers and cheese for the rest of her life and be perfectly happy! She also liked eating while doing something else because she would sometimes forget about her food worries, and that was nice.

Food issues

Toddlers are often picky eaters and food battles are common. Anxious toddlers are also normally picky eaters, but they bring an array of other mealtime issues that can be confusing, mysterious and frustrating! Food issues can range from mildly annoying to medically concerning. There are some toddlers who have serious eating issues that impede their development and growth. These are children who would indeed "starve to death" if professional intervention was not obtained. There are feeding therapists and special feeding clinics to support these acute feeding issues, but this subject is not addressed here. Those medically concerning feeding issues are beyond the scope of this book and require ongoing professional support. If you are not sure if your toddler has a serious feeding issue I encourage you to see a child therapist, feeding therapist or a speech and language pathologist for an initial assessment and further guidance.

Some anxious toddlers have ongoing feeding struggles, but they are not losing weight and they are not nutritionally deprived. Their feeding issues are still scary, they still worry parents and they still need to be addressed! In this chapter I have outlined the most common feeding issues anxious toddlers face.

Textures and sensory issues

If you have an anxious toddler, they are much more likely to have sensory integration issues. We will talk in more detail about what these are and how to address them in Chapter 11. Sensory issues, in general, relate to a hypo- or hyperreactivity to various senses. In Chapter 11 I will address issues with oral hyper- and hyposensitivity in more detail.

In our vignette with Kate, she was exhibiting hypersensitivity to oral input. Textures were more prominent in her mouth and her gag reflex was much more easily triggered. This sensitivity to textures made it hard for her to eat foods that had mixed textures. She also had a hard time with food textures that didn't fully dissolve in her mouth. She would feel anxious if she sensed too much food was in her mouth. She was overwhelmed with new smells and tastes and was reluctant to try new foods.

Further complicating this were her tactile sensitivities. She was unable to handle the sensation of sticky or gloppy substances on her hands or face. Kate's way of coping with her sensitivities was to avoid chewy foods that did not fully dissolve and to let food fall out of her mouth when she felt she was at sensory overload. She would demand her hands be cleaned when she could no longer handle the feeling of stickiness on her body.

Some toddlers have other sensory issues related to temperature. What might seem lukewarm to us, might feel burning hot to an orally sensitive child. You might find yourself shuttling your child's food from the microwave to the freezer before they are content with the correct temperature.

Some toddlers have oral *hypo*sensitivities. In my experience I have found anxious toddlers more often have oral *hyper*sensitivities. A child with oral hyposensitivities is less sensitive to input in their mouth. These children tend to over stuff their mouth until their cheeks puff out. They pocket their food like little chipmunks and are not overwhelmed by the large quantity of food filling their cheeks. They have a harder time *feeling* their food and are at a greater risk of choking. They crave strong flavors and are more likely to try new foods. These children often drool or have excessive saliva build-up, commonly due to low oral muscle tone.

If your child is showing strong oral defensiveness (such as gagging or throwing up), it would probably be most beneficial to, at a minimum, get an evaluation from a speech and language pathologist (SLP) who specializes in feeding and sensory issues. A speech therapist can assess the functionality of how your toddler is eating and what areas need to be strengthened and/or desensitized. Some children do not chew their food, and swallow most if it whole. Other children avoid having food touch certain areas of the mouth. An SLP would have the skill to assess where your child's struggles lie and how to address them. They can also show you how to do oral exercises with your child that will help them overcome their oral sensitivities.

When trying to help your child adapt to eating solid foods, begin by observing their eating habits and identifying their safe foods. What type of textures feel safe to them? Do they like hard, crunchy food or smooth, mushy food? Do they gag on everything or just mixed textures? Do they have an aversion to messy play? Do they get upset when their hands get dirty?

Exposing your child to messy play can help their eating habits. When you are a toddler, eating is a messy ordeal! If your child can't handle mess, they won't be able to successfully eat a full range of foods. You can introduce your child to edible messy play. Have your child finger paint with pudding or whipped cream. You can put different food coloring, powdered jello or Kool-Aid into whipped cream to give your child an array of edible "finger paint" colors. Initially, have your child finger paint on construction paper, but eventually put them in their highchair and have them paint directly on their tray with their fingers. Encourage your toddler to lick their fingers. Paint along with your toddler and lick your fingers as well, showing them that the paint is alright to eat. Make sure you say, "This is special yummy paint that we can eat!" in an effort to prevent them from thinking all paint should be licked! Putting them in a place where they eat, like a highchair, helps further highlight the acceptance of eating and licking their paint in that context.

If your toddler is not ready for messy play, you can have them play in a bin of beans, rice or kinetic sand that won't stick to their fingers. This helps give your toddler alternative sensations on their hands without the anxiety of anything sticking to them. Once they have adapted to this type of play, you can slowly move to messier play. Sometimes, initially having messy play in the bath can be less anxiety-producing because they can wash their hands as soon as they feel overwhelmed.

Take your toddler's lead on how quickly you move from one step to another. If you see your child getting more anxious and overwhelmed—or worse, they gag or throw up when you try these desensitizing exercises—it is probably a sign that they would benefit from a feeding therapist.

Another way to help your child's feeding is to get them to adapt to more sensations in their mouth. You can use textured spoons while feeding your child smooth food. This will help your child adapt to mixed textured food without the bumps staying in their mouth. You can find textured spoons online through many therapeutic catalogs and stores. Another way to desensitize your child's mouth is to use vibrating toys and toothbrushes. Like the textured spoons, you can find an array of oral therapeutic tools online, including textured and vibrating oral motor tools. Some children have to build up a tolerance to a strong vibrating toy. You can dip the toothbrush or toy into something the child enjoys eating to encourage them to put it in their mouth. In a perfect world, it is better to let your toddler control the vibrating toothbrush and place it in their mouth independently. If this does not occur and you fear it never will, you can slowly encourage this behavior by lightly placing it on their lips.

If you worry about your child getting a balanced diet with the type of food texture they prefer, you can alter their food to fit their preferred texture. If your child prefers smooth foods, you can puree vegetables and fruit. If your child likes crunchy foods, you can make veggie or fruit chips by baking slices of fruits and vegetables. You can buy freeze-dried food to serve fruits and vegetables with a crunchier and less mushy texture. You can buy a home dehydrator or freeze dryer to freeze dry your own food, although they can be pretty pricey! The ultimate goal is to have your child adapt to a variety of textures, but in the interim you will feel better if you know they are still having a balanced diet.

Engaging your child in fun play around food will help minimize their anxiety about feeding. You can use silly songs and fun stories that animate the food and turn it into characters. Incorporating a story that involves eating the objects in the story can encourage consumption. You can order edible eyes easily online (usually used for cupcakes) and turn their food into talking characters that encourage them to eat. Yo Gabba Gabba! has a wonderful song called *Party in My Tummy* that is about various foods wanting to join the party in the tummy. This would be a fun song to play while doing food play, as it encourages eating animated foods.

If your child doesn't like touching their food, get them to use colorful toothpicks and chopsticks to pick up their food. This can be turned into a game. You can play matching games such as, "Can you use the red toothpick to pick up the red strawberry?" and "Can you use the blue toothpick to pick up the blueberry?" Food play doesn't have to end in your child eating the food. The goal is to expose them to various foods and get them at least to interact with them.

Play food games with a prize box. Fill up a treasure box with small prizes you can find at the dollar store. Have a "texture challenge" where a child has to "kiss" a food they would not usually put in their mouth. If you want to make it more fun, use the edible eyes for the foods in the challenge. Exposing your child to the sensations of various textures on their lips is the first step to desensitizing them. As they progress, you can have challenges that include placing the food in their mouth (with permission to spit it out) and eventually swallowing it. At the start of the game, it would be helpful to use the vibrating toothbrush on your child to prepare their mouth for new textures and make their mouth less sensitive.

Food battles and picky eaters

You may wonder how your toddler survives based on the amount they eat! Considering your child's stomach is the size of their fist, they don't have much to fill. Toddlers can be notoriously picky! As discussed above, anxious toddlers are often more sensitive to taste, texture and temperature. They discover the foods that are "safe" and they stick with them. These are usually foods that are slightly more bland, easy to chew and easy to swallow. Common toddler favorites include crackers (e.g. Goldfish), dry cereal (Cheerios), chicken nuggets (often processed meat) and macaroni and cheese. These are foods that are easy to eat and do not have a broad range of intense flavors.

Unfortunately, fruits, vegetables and chewy meats are not some of the most popular toddler foods! Anxious toddlers tend to have an even harder time with these foods because they have varied textures and can have intense flavors (especially fruits). Chewy meats do not fully dissolve and are harder to swallow. Vegetables often present an array of textures and can have a more bitter taste.

Understanding why your child is picky is an important element in helping to address this situation. Parents' perceptions of what is causing the problem can be skewed around this topic. Some parents think their child is just being stubborn and those who view feeding in this way will often get into food battles. A food battle is like a stand off between child and parent. Even if the parent "wins" the battle, they will lose the war.

When you put pressure on your child to eat, you are adding a secondary stressor that will further exacerbate the problem. Now, not only does your child worry about what they are eating, they also worry about *your* reaction to what they eat. This is not a successful approach with the anxious toddler. I have worked with families who have set timers, tried spanking and forced children to sit at the table long after a meal was over. Usually those situations ended with the child vomiting, never eating that food again and/or acting out at the next meal.

With childhood obesity at an all time high, it is also important that you teach your child how to detect when they are full and satiated. You want your child to verbalize when they are done with their meal, even if their plate isn't clean. Allowing your child the control of ending their own meal will teach them that eating ends when their stomach registers fullness and not when they eat everything in front of them. To help your child feel success, put small portions on their plate. It is better for them to ask for more than for you to feel as if you are throwing most of the food away.

Parents with a "clean your plate" mentality are typically just emulating the parenting approach used on them when they were children. Some parents might feel, "If it was good enough for me, it should be good enough for them!" However, your anxious toddler may not be like you. They are not being picky on purpose and most anxious toddlers want to appease their parents, not anger them. Instead of getting into a control battle, it is more productive and effective to try and fix the origin of the problem. The origin of the problem is not "How can I upset my parent?" The origin centers on fear.

The child is fearful of new tastes, textures and smells. You can see your child's trepidation if they smell or lightly lick their food before they venture to eat it.

One way to "stack the deck" in your favor is to present foods separately rather than mix them together. If you are making a chicken casserole for instance, your child is more likely to eat it if you put the chicken in one pile and the vegetables in another pile. If you are making tacos, put the ground beef on one side of the plate and the taco shell on the other side. When food is mixed together, the presentation is scary and mysterious. When possible, make a more simplistic version of what everyone else is having, or leave the sauce off. When you put the plate in front of your child, tell them what you are serving them. This helps demystify the meal and enables them to build their food vocabulary. You want your child to have words for the foods they like and dislike, so they can communicate what they prefer in the future.

Some parents may feel as if altering their meal is accommodating their child's food issues. Parents might have the mentality of, "You eat what I serve you or you don't eat at all." Unfortunately, these children would not eat at all. Instead of viewing food issues as a battle, view them more as a teaching experience. You have to help your child adjust to various textures and flavors. Once they experience success, they are more likely to branch out and take new risks. If you prepare your usual meal with some minor adjustments, you might change the outcome of your mealtime success.

Some children don't even like their food touching! I have worked with children who would not touch anything on their plate once they saw their meat was touching their vegetables. Eventually you will teach your child to adapt and eat food that is touching, but you need to pick your battles. Once your child will eat a healthy, balanced diet, then you can tackle rigidity around touching food.

Do not decide for your child what they won't eat. Even if you absolutely know your toddler will never eat the meal you are serving the rest of the family, put a small spoonful on their plate too. Adapt the food into a more simplistic form if possible. Toddlers have to be repeatedly exposed to new foods before they decide they like them. By placing that new food on their plate, you are exposing your child to the smell and look of something new. They might eventually give the new food a sniff and even a lick.

It is helpful always to have some food on their plate that is part of their "safe" foods. A child will feel more successful at mealtime if there is something on their plate that they are confident to eat. For dinner, this might be a side dish of rice, noodles or macaroni and cheese. They can join the rest of the family, eating what they are comfortable with while being exposed to some new foods too.

When you have the time—and patience—let your little one help you cook. When your child helps you cook, they are more vested in the meal and they are more likely to try the food. Your child will take pride in what they made and there will be less mystery about what is in it. Even if they do not eat the final product, you are exposing your child to the smells and textures of the food as they cook it.

If you are concerned about the level of balance and nutrition your toddler is receiving, talk to your pediatrician about supplements. Some parents will give their children a supplemental milkshake or an enriched toddler formula to ensure they are getting all the nutrients they need. Unfortunately, these drinks can be filling, so toddlers tend to eat even less food when they have them, but you have to weigh up the pros against the cons.

Anxieties around eating

Toddlers can have anxiety around eating for various reasons besides oral sensitivities. If a toddler has medical issues such as reflux, food allergies or celiac disease they are more likely to have heightened anxiety around eating in general. Any association with food and pain can make a child more anxious and avoidant of eating.

Some children have a fear of choking, sometimes caused by a history of choking. Anxious parents can cause an increased fear of choking in their children by verbalizing their fears to their child. Parents might say things like, "Be careful, you might choke" and "Take small bites so you don't choke." Some anxious children will internalize their parent's fear and make the fear their own.

For the anxious eater, distraction might be the most effective answer. When a child ruminates over their food's texture or they are afraid they might choke or be in pain, it is better to have them focus on something else. I have worked with children who will chew their food for five to ten minutes before they get the courage to swallow it. They fear they haven't chewed the food up enough and that they might choke. Other children might fixate on the fear of getting sick from what they are eating. Ironically, all that worrying while eating will exacerbate any indigestion. Having the television on while your child eats has been a big no-no in the bible of "how to be a perfect parent." Unfortunately, sometimes what is good for kids is not always what is good for *your* kid. Putting the TV on or playing music or games will distract your child from their anxious thoughts and help them be more productive eaters. When your child has ongoing success with eating, you can scale back the distractions.

I have worked with toddlers who are afraid to go to the bathroom (we will discuss bathroom issues in Chapter 5). Some highly intelligent toddlers realize that what goes in, must come out, and those who know that eating will eventually make them poop can develop a fear of eating. If your toddler has both eating and bathroom issues, it is important to establish if there is a link. In order to address this type of feeding issue, you must start with fixing the toileting fear.

Another common feeding issue to address is the fear of eating in front of others. There are toddlers who are acutely shy and may not even speak in front of other people. They become embarrassed when other people see them eat. They may refuse to eat at a friend's house or at daycare/pre-school. In the short term, this may not seem like a big problem, but when the child goes to school all day this becomes a serious issue.

You can help reframe your child's worries by telling them that eating is normal and that everyone eats in front of other people. You can invite one friend they are close to and have them eat a meal together at your home. When your child is comfortable with this, have your child eat a meal at their home. Slowly add more children to the playdate to help desensitize your child. If your child is resistant, you can set up a "challenge" where they earn a prize for eating in front their friends.

Mealtime rigidity

As we discussed in the first chapter, anxious toddlers tend to be rigid. They want things done a certain way and can become inflexible to change. When toddlers are anxious, they will become even more rigid in their behavior. You will notice an increase in rigidity if your toddler has feeding issues.

Toddlers want their favorite cups and plates, their special place at the table and their food served in a certain way. When you veer from these routines, anxious toddlers can have a complete meltdown. Although we all love our routines, anxious toddlers *need* their routine. This unhealthy dependence on routines can become debilitating and dysfunctional.

In order to help your child become more flexible, change your routine as often as you can. Try to use a variety of plates and cups. Cut your child's sandwich in different ways (in four one day and in half another day). Play musical chairs at dinner and have everyone sit in a different spot. Although this may seem like an odd approach, it will help your child adapt to different environments as they get older.

Some routines can be a positive aspect of mealtime. Having everyone sit down together for dinner time is a wonderful family tradition that can begin at a young age. Even if your child doesn't eat the meal put in front of them, it is nice to establish "family time" around dinner. Older toddlers can be taught to clear their own plate and to ask to be excused from the table. Even though their behavior won't be perfect, you can start to teach your child the structure of family mealtime.

Some toddlers do not have the capability to sit still, as we will discuss in the next section, and you may have to delay this tradition until it is not painful! Don't beat yourself up if you have a vision of how you want things to go and it doesn't go that way. Parents need to be flexible too!

Wiggle, wiggle watch me giggle!

Toddlers do not like to sit still. This can make mealtime difficult and frustrating. If there is anxiety around eating, your child might become even more hyperactive. Hyperactivity is sometimes not about high energy, but rather a by-product of anxiety and hyperarousal.

Parents have different expectations about table manners but it is important to be realistic about how long you require your child to sit for a meal. If your child is exceptionally wiggly and it is interfering with their ability to eat, it might be better to keep them in a highchair for as long as you can. Some families have a small table and chairs where their child can eat. This is a great way to teach your child independence, especially for breakfast and lunch. In a perfect world, it would be nice to include your toddler at the main table for dinner, even if they last only five or ten minutes. Including them at dinner, even for a brief period of time, helps them to acclimatize to a regular mealtime routine and to feel like part of the family.

To maximize your toddler's stay at any table, have their food ready before you call them to eat. Toddlers are impatient and if they have to spend five or ten minutes waiting for their food or waiting for their food to cool down, they will be ready to get up before the meal even begins! Having some finger foods on their plate can also help the meal to be more successful. Children will typically eat finger foods quicker and, if they are feeling tired, they may not even try the challenge of a spoon or fork.

To snack or not to snack? That is the question

A big question many parents ask is, "Do I limit my toddler's snacking?" Like many things in parenting, there is no right or wrong answer. There is not one definitive parenting approach; children thrive and flourish with many different approaches. You have to assess your child's personality and needs and determine what works best for you!

Some parents feel that if they limit their child's snacking during the day, they tend to eat a larger quantity during meals. Other parents feel their children eat a larger quantity when they are allowed to snack throughout the day. If your child has an increased level of anxiety around sit-down meals and doesn't ever seem to eat much, snacking might be a good option. Putting high protein snacks on their small table throughout the day may increase your child's calorie intake. If your child does not consume a large amount at sit-down mealtimes, limiting their snacking might improve their appetite. It is important to remember that, regardless of which approach you take, toddlers have small stomachs and can only digest a small amount of food in one sitting.

· · · · · · · · · · · · · · · · ·

CHAPTER 4

Bedtime Disasters

Monica and George

Monica and George have been sleep deprived ever since their cute little son Tanner entered the world. Tanner has had a hard time self-soothing ever since he was an infant. Early on, Monica would rock Tanner to sleep while she breastfed; she would get him to fall asleep on the breast and then carefully lie him down in his crib. He would sometimes wake with a start when he felt her putting him down and he would start to cry. Monica would then pick him up and get him to latch on to her breast while rocking him back to sleep again. Sometimes she would get so tired that she would just hold him while they both slept.

When Tanner was a baby, he woke up frequently during the night to breastfeed. Initially, Monica and George had a crib next to their bed, but with all the frequent feedings they felt it was easier just to have him sleep with them. They thought once Tanner was a little bit older, they would move him into his own room. Unfortunately that was going to be more of a struggle than they anticipated.

Eventually, Tanner turned two and he stopped breastfeeding, but he still needed his mom and dad to help put him to bed. He was also, much to their dismay, still in their bed. They had made a big deal about decorating his room using his favorite Disney character as a theme and they even ordered a bed in the shape of a car. Unfortunately, all their efforts did little to entice him to sleep in his own room. Usually Tanner would start in their bed and they would pat his back and rub his hair until he fell asleep. They would then carry him to his bedroom and put him in his toddler bed. A few hours later, Tanner would wake up screaming and demand to sleep in their bed. He would insist that someone lie down with him until he fell asleep. His mom would lie down with him in her bed and the same cycle would repeat. When Tanner was asleep he would be carried back to his bedroom again. Usually Tanner would then sleep until around 3 or 4am, when he would frantically come running down the hall and back into his parents' bed. At that point, his parents were generally exhausted and would let him sleep the rest of the night with them. This disruptive sleep routine became their norm for almost a year.

When Tanner turned three, Monica gave birth to their second child, Anna. Tanner's disruptive sleep habits were starting to affect their new baby's sleep. They had Anna's crib in their bedroom and Tanner would frequently wake her up when he was lying in their bed. Monica and George didn't want to have both children sleeping in their room. They eventually got Tanner at least to begin the night in his own bedroom. Monica would lie down with him in his room and would pat and rub his head until he fell asleep. Sometimes he would startle when he felt her getting up and he would cry, insisting that she continued to lie with him. There were many nights when Monica would just fall asleep in his bed with him. This became an issue for Monica and George's relationship, as they rarely got any alone time together.

As Tanner got more expressive, he would talk about his fears of shadows in his room and of scary monsters that might eat him. His parents assured him they would keep him safe, but that did nothing to quell his fears. He insisted on keeping his bedroom light on and he said the nightlight wasn't bright enough. Before he went to bed at night he would line up his stuffed animals on his bed and would get upset if his mom accidentally bumped one out of position. He wanted his mom to check his bed for bugs and liked her to smooth out his sheets so there were no wrinkles. His evening routine seemed to keep growing bigger and more rigid.

Tanner would occasionally have bad dreams where he would wake up screaming, "No!" During those times it was hard to get him to fully wake up. He would often cry for 15–20 minutes before he could be settled back down. He was never able to articulate what his dreams were about and when his parents asked him about it in the morning he never seemed to remember.

When Tanner turned three and a half, George got a promotion that required him to travel often. Maria didn't feel comfortable at night and would often let Tanner sleep in their bed for those "special nights." Tanner slept well those nights and didn't have his normal nighttime awakenings. When George came back, Tanner was angry and resentful. He would beg his mom to let him sleep in their bed, but his mom would tell him it wasn't a "special night."

●●●●●●

Tanner

When Tanner was a baby he loved the feeling of warm milk in his mouth as he was rocked to sleep. The sensation soothed him and he knew it was safe and comfortable to go to sleep. When the rocking stopped and he felt the coldness of not being pressed against his mom, he would wake up and worry that his mother was no longer with him. Usually he would be picked up and enveloped in the warmth of his mom's arms again and he would be soothed into a state of sleep once more. He woke up often and didn't know what to do. He would cry and would be filled with warm milk once again. Many times he wasn't hungry, but he enjoyed the comfort of breastfeeding and it would help him go back to sleep.

When Tanner got a little older they made a special room just for him. He thought the room was so cool! However, he didn't understand why they wanted him to sleep in there. No matter *how cool he thought his room was, he would never want to be away from his mom and dad. They were so far away! Tanner still needed to feel the warmth of his mom close to him. Patting his back had replaced the rocking, but it was just as rhythmic and soothing. He liked when his mom massaged his head before he went to sleep. He could not imagine going to sleep without his mom doing those things to help him relax. Most nights Tanner would wake up and find himself alone in his bedroom! That was scary for him. How could this happen? He would be sleeping in his parents' room all cozy and would wake to find himself alone in his room. This upset Tanner and he didn't know why his parents kept insisting that he didn't sleep with them. Usually by the third or fourth time his parents would realize that they really wanted him to sleep with them and they would stop moving him back to his room.*

When Tanner's little baby sister came home, his parents seemed even more insistent that he sleep in his own room. Why did they let his baby sister sleep in their room, but not him? It seemed as if they just didn't care as much about him! His parents seemed tired and less patient with him. He sometimes got yelled at and they shouted at him that he was going to wake up the baby. To him it seemed as if that was all they cared about!

Eventually his parents realized he wasn't going to go to sleep on his own and they stopped trying. His mom would lie with him in his bed and would pat his back and rub his head. Although it wasn't as nice as his parents' bed, having his mom lie with him made him feel better. He would try to keep his eyes open as long as he could because he knew his mom would try and sneak out. Why didn't she just go to bed with him? She would do that some nights. Most of the time, fatigue got the best of him, his eyes got heavy and he'd start to fall asleep. The moment he heard the creak of his bed as his mom stood, his eyes would pop open! He'd tell his mom not to leave and she'd lie back down with him. If he did this a few times, his mom would eventually fall asleep in his bed and then he would relax.

As Tanner got a little bit older, his room started to scare him. There were scary shadows on the walls that looked like monsters just waiting to grab him! He was afraid of what might be under his bed and in his closet. His parents kept telling him that he was safe because they were there to protect him, but then they would leave! Who was going to protect him when he was left alone in his room?

Tanner also got increasingly worried about bugs in his bed. He once thought he saw a black dot that looked as if it could have been a bug. Sometimes when he slept he saw bugs all over his bed, but when he woke up they weren't there. He wasn't sure where they went or how they disappeared. He would make his mom shake out his blanket and smooth his sheets to assure him there were no bugs each night. He'd also line up his stuffed animals to keep guard in case any bugs tried to get on his bed. This made him feel better. He also felt better if his light stayed on so he could see what was in his bed and ensure that he saw no shadows. The bright light made it hard for him to tell when it was morning or when it was time to get up, but he didn't care.

For some reason Tanner's dad started not sleeping at home some nights. His mom called those nights "special nights" and he was allowed to sleep in her bed the whole night! He loved "special nights" because he didn't have to worry about her leaving his room and he never worried about shadows or bugs in her bed! When his dad came home he would be mad. Why couldn't he sleep in their bed when his dad was home! His dad seemed to get mad at his mom for letting him sleep in their bed. Tanner didn't know why he cared, he wasn't even there. The nights after his "special night" were much harder. His fears seemed to intensify and he had an even harder time falling asleep. He would cry and beg for his mom to let him sleep back in her bed, but his dad insisted this did not happen.

Parenting style

It's important to discuss parenting styles and beliefs before getting too deep into this chapter. Every family has different practices, based on belief systems and on their particular culture. Many families believe in the closeness of sharing a bed or a bedroom. These are parental and cultural decisions and they are not based on their child's anxious disposition. These families may not be concerned with their child's need to sleep with them and they may not identify this as an issue.

Other parents may have wanted their infant to sleep in their room initially, but did not expect their child to still be in their bedroom past infancy. These parents are continuing to have their child sleep in their bed out of necessity and *not* based on a belief system. There are no right or wrong answers here, although many with strong opinions may disagree. We all need to be accepting of different parenting approaches and not criticize or judge those who do things differently from us. Each family should do what resonates with them and what makes them feel the most comfortable. This section aims to help parents who have their child sleeping with them, but would prefer to have their child sleep in their own room.

Some parents give up the battle of having their own bed and think that their child will "grow out of it." They won't. If anxiety is driving the need for your child to sleep next to you, they will not grow out of this problem. I have worked with teenagers who are still sleeping in their parents' bed. Anxious children will need to be taught the tools to sleep independently or they will *always* want to sleep with you.

Fall asleep with me!

In order to look at why your toddler is afraid to fall asleep without you, we have to look at the origin of the problem. Many parents don't realize that they started creating their child's sleep habits when their child was just an infant. Parents who nursed and rocked their infants until their child completely went to sleep inadvertently caused their young children to become dependent on those actions to *fall* asleep. When a baby is put into their crib while not being fully asleep, they are quicker to learn how to self-sooth. These infants develop sleep habits that do not depend on being fed, rocked or held. For most babies this is not a problem and they will eventually be able to transition from this dependency to independency without an issue, but the anxious child is less likely to adapt. Unfortunately, the skill of self-soothing is not learned when a child is always quickly soothed by a parent and so it will have to be taught in toddlerhood.

As shown in the vignette that opened this chapter, rocking and breastfeeding usually move to patting and massaging. There is nothing wrong with patting your child or giving them a relaxing massage before they fall asleep. The key, if you are trying to help your toddler sleep more independently, is to not put your child down fully asleep. What does that mean? It means purposefully ending your tuck-in before your child is fully asleep. You actually want them to be aware of when you are leaving. Yes, that may seem counterintuitive, as you are going to have a startled and upset toddler, but you can't teach them to self-sooth if they are already asleep.

Where to begin? Is your child still sleeping in your bed and you want to help them sleep in their own bed? Getting your child to sleep in their own room independently is a slow and patient process. These habits were not created overnight and they will not change that quickly either. The first step is getting them to fall asleep independent of your touch. If you pat or massage your child until they fall asleep, begin by doing this for just a few minutes and then lie down with them without touching them until they are fast asleep. This will slowly teach your child that they do not need your touch to soothe themselves into sleep.

If your child needs to hold your hand or have physical contact with you throughout the night, try to move positions so they are not getting the physical reassurance that you are there. This will help them adapt when they are in their own bed and do not have you right next to them. Once you have mastered not soothing or physically touching your child throughout the night, you can move them to a cot or a blow-up mattress next to your bed. This will help your child get the feel of having a twin-sized mattress all to themselves. Eventually you will want to place the cot as far away from your bed as possible, giving your child a sense of independence while they are still able to see you.

The next jump is the big one. Unfortunately, there is no small step from your bedroom to their bedroom. For older toddlers you can have a treasure box full of little trinkets and toys that they can earn for being brave and sleeping in their own room. Let them decorate the box and pick out the prizes themselves—this will help them be more vested in the challenge. You can explain to your child that you know staying in their own room can be scary and that they can earn a treasure in the morning for being brave. This is not going to make the process easy, but it makes it at least a little more enticing for your child. Let them pick out a treasure, even if they didn't fully succeed, and point out the times they were brave and worked through their fears.

If your child has issues sleeping in their room or has anxiety at night, do not use their room for time out. Any negative connotation associated with their room will further deter them from wanting to sleep in there. You want them to associate happy thoughts and feelings with their room. Decorating the room in the style your child would find inviting and fun will create this positive association. It will not in itself make them want to sleep there, but it will make the room more enticing, and you'll need all the help you can get!

Put your child to bed as you did when they were in your room, patting or rubbing them until they are sleepy, but not fully asleep. Initially you will probably have to stay in the room until your toddler goes to bed. Baby steps are crucial for a smooth transition. Once you are done patting your child, tell them you will stay in their room, but not on their bed. Sit in the door frame, but do not interact with or talk to your toddler. You can tell them firmly, "If you talk to me or get out of your bed, I will not sit here *while* you fall asleep." Be careful to not say "*until* you fall asleep" or they will be fearful of falling asleep, anticipating that you will be leaving when that occurs.

After you have been doing the above for a while with complete success, move outside the door frame into the hall while they are falling asleep. You can tell your toddler that you are teaching them to fall asleep on their own and that the next step is for you to wait out in the hall. Be sure to be out of their eyesight, as this is the major difference for this next step. It is not uncommon for children to call for their parent or to sneak into the hall to make sure their parent is still there. Remind your child that you will not stay in the hall if they talk or get out of their bed. You might have to do this once or twice for them to take you seriously. Do not leave the hall until you know they are fully asleep. Having your child sneak out of bed to find you gone will not help this process and some trust will be lost.

After a period of time your child should begin to fall asleep faster, having learned to self-sooth. The next step is periodic check-ins. You can tell your child that you are going to be sitting on the couch or in your bed, but you will periodically check in on them. Space these check-ins further and further apart, until you are just checking in once before you go to bed. Sometimes giving your older toddler a walkie talkie can help them feel more connected to you. Teach them how to talk to you from another room. You can tell them, "When you are scared, you can talk to me on the walkie talkie." You could also get a camera with a feature that enables you to talk through the monitor. This helps reassure them that you are able to see them and that they are not alone. It is also comforting for your child to be able to speak to you in a low voice and still be heard. They develop a trust that you will come to them when they need you and that even though they are alone, you are still *present* with them.

The process of moving your anxious toddler out of your room and successfully to their room will take time. The time will vary depending on the child and even the parent's level of comfort. You don't want to rush things, but you also don't want to take steps back. Once you have managed success, do not go back to old habits out of comfort or convenience. Tackling sleep issues is a tiring battle for all parents and there is a high risk of parents "relapsing" due to fatigue, guilt or both! At the end of the day you are giving your child the gift of self-reliance that will help them as young adults when they live on their own. The older children I have talked to who need their parents to lie down with them have voiced embarrassment and shame. There is a sense of pride and empowerment in children who are no longer afraid to go to sleep and can happily fall asleep on their own.

Some parents I have worked with have discovered through this process, that *they* are actually the ones who got reassurance from their child sleeping with them and *they* do not feel comfortable when their child is sleeping without them. Sometimes spouses differ on whether their child sleeping with them is even a problem at all. Sometimes halfway through this process, one spouse will announce that they didn't have a problem with the sleeping arrangement and were only doing it to make their partner happy. In order not to confuse your child, fully explore your level of commitment to and comfort in moving your child out of your room. If you feel as if your child is not safe if you are not lying next to them and you wish you didn't feel that way, you might want to explore this issue further in therapy for yourself.

If a parent goes out of town or travels often, do not confuse your child by letting them sleep in your bed. A typical child without anxiety can adapt to these special nights, but an anxious child will have a hard time going back to their room after the "treat" is over. Often this happens if the other spouse is not fully on board with the plan or if they have their own anxieties over sleeping alone.

I have worked with many parents who have given up halfway through this process. It is tiring and exhausting and some children will fight you the entire way. Try to stay the course and know that the payoff will be worth it in the end!

Fears at night

It is important to realize that fears in anxious toddlers are not usually based on actual experiences or traumatic events. I have worked with parents who are baffled by why their toddler is afraid for their safety. They will assure me that nothing bad has ever happened to their child, so they can't understand why their child is so afraid. Anxiety manifests in predictable ways and with predictable fears. Common fears for toddlers include the dark, shadows, monsters, bad guys, bugs, storms and fire. The fears of anxious children are all similar, regardless of their family lifestyle or their varied life experiences.

One of the biggest struggles for anxious toddlers is their nighttime fears. As toddlers become more aware of the world around them, their fears start to develop as well. The imagination of the toddler starts to grow as their cognitive abilities expand. What was once just a shadow is now a scary monster waiting to eat them!

Toddlers are fearful of various dangers in their bedroom. It is important to try and assess what makes your toddler fearful. Ask your toddler what scares them. Ask them probing questions such as, "What are you afraid might happen to you in your room?" Older toddlers can usually articulate their fears when they are asked the right questions and are given enough time. Ask open-ended questions and avoid closed-ended questions that put ideas in your toddler's head. For example an open-ended question would be something like, "What's the scariest thing in your room?" A closed-ended question would be something like, "Are you afraid of monsters in your room?" They may not have been afraid of monsters before you asked the question, but they might be after you asked! You don't want to lead your toddler with your own assumptions of what may be scary to them.

Knowing what your toddler is scared of will help you reframe their thinking. A general sweeping statement like, "There is nothing to be afraid of" will have little effect on your anxious toddler. Addressing their specific fear and reframing their misperceptions is more likely to be successful. Also, telling your child, "Don't worry we are here to protect you" can ironically increase your child's fear! Although it is a common reassurance parents give their children, it can validate the idea that there is something the child needs *protecting* from. It is much more effective to address directly the specific fear and to reassure them that they are safe.

Some fears might be based on what they have seen on TV. Anxious toddlers are very sensitive to what they watch on TV. Shows that seem completely uplifting and harmless might have components or themes that somehow scare them. I have worked with children who have found shows like *Peter Rabbit* and *Dora the Explorer* scary! If you see that your toddler is hiding their eyes or recoiling while watching a TV show, pay attention to what is happening in the story. Tell your child things like, "Peter Rabbit is going to be okay. He is always okay at the end of each story." Help your child gauge whether shows are too scary for them. If they are covering their eyes you might say something like, "This show is scary for you, huh?" and ask them, "Can we watch something that doesn't scare you?"

If your toddler is afraid of shadows at night, take a flashlight and show them how shadows are made. Have fun with shadow puppets and shadow play. Go through their room with the lights off and check out what shadows are on their walls. If possible, move toys and stuffed animals to eliminate as many shadows as you can. Some nightlights produce a greater number of shadows than others—try to find one that provides maximum light with limited shadows. Some fiber optic lights produce fewer shadows than the average nightlight. Go through the room with your toddler and show them what objects are making the shadows you cannot eliminate. Interact with the shadows by moving the object or putting your hands through it so they see the origin of the shadow.

If your toddler is afraid of monsters, ask them to draw the monster. You can then get a better picture of what their fear is based on. Sometimes they are afraid of the teeth or the claws and other times it is the size of the monster. When watching TV you can start pointing out to them what is real and what is pretend. When watching cartoons, tell your child it is pretend and not real. Young toddlers have no ability to delineate reality from fantasy, but as your toddler gets older they will start developing this skill. When you help your child identify what is real and what is not real you are helping plant the seeds for future reframing. These seeds will bloom in the long run and will be very helpful. In the short run, toddlers will hold onto their beliefs in fantasy and will not be appeased by your reassurances that it isn't real. I would suggest not feeding into your child's fantasies by doing things like "monster spray" (where a pretend spray deters monsters) or by making signs that say "No monsters allowed." These approaches are cute, but they run the risk of validating your child's fears that monsters *are* real and have the potential to increase their anxiety.

You can use a calming spray or oil, such as lavender, which is used in aromatherapy to combat anxiety and is thought to encourage relaxation. You can tell your child that the oil will help them have "happy thoughts" and can help keep the "scary thoughts" away. It is very similar to the concept of the monster spray, without aligning yourself with your toddler's fear.

Soft music or a sound machine can also be helpful. Background noise helps your child be less hypervigilant to the sounds of the house. Every time an anxious toddler hears a noise outside their room, their imagination is triggered. You can eliminate that issue by having soothing sounds in their room. You can have the music on a loop so they are listening to a constant sound. There are sleep CDs that have delta waves playing under the music that will encourage relaxation. Playing the same music each night will eventually have a Pavlovian response—your child will start to get sleepy when they hear their sleep CD being played. It is best to avoid keeping the TV on for background noise and light. Although it is initially distracting and comforting for the child, TV is stimulating the brain and providing their mind with input that they are still processing even as they sleep. TV is also a bad sleep habit that is hard to break once it has been established—so better not to start it at all!

When your child is afraid there is something or someone hiding in their room, it is helpful to "play detective" with them. Teach your child to face their fears by checking their room if they are scared. If you discovered that one of their fears was a monster hiding in their closet or under their bed, have the child check. If they are too scared, have them watch while you check. This helps alleviate the fear that there is something lurking in their room. It also teaches them how to face their fears alone when they are a little bit older. If there are any dolls, clowns or puppets that can be construed as creepy or scary, they might be better off living in another room. There are lots of fears around dolls, especially as kids get older and are exposed to trailers for scary movies like *Chucky* or *Annabelle*.

Keeping the closet door closed at night is helpful. Any black cracks (such as a door slightly ajar) can be triggering for anxious children. Regarding the bedroom door, some kids insist that it be kept wide open and some want it fully shut. If they want their bedroom door open, it helps to keep the hall light on, eliminating the fear of the ominous black crack.

As discussed in the opening vignette, some toddlers are afraid of bugs in their room. Help them "play detective" and have them look around the room and on their bed for bugs. If they are unable to do this themselves, have them watch you do it. Playing detective helps children learn to be proactive with their fears, as they take control of the situation and calm their anxiety. Watch your own reaction to bugs, as many of us have an extreme reaction to them ourselves! Our children watch us and take their cue from us on what is safe and what is not. If they see us screaming and standing on a chair, they will probably assume bugs are pretty dangerous.

Storms can make even a calm toddler feel anxious. Loud thunderstorms and intense lightening can be scary, especially at bedtime. Explain thunder and lightening in basic words to your child. Although it is cute to tell your toddler things like "God is bowling," I would recommend sticking with basic facts. You want your child to trust your explanations and not question what you have told them as they get a little older. This is especially true of the anxious toddler, who will remember everything you ever told them! Explain to them that the trees and plants need the rain and that they are being fed. Have your child play out in the rain when it seems safe. Encouraging rain or puddle play will help take the stigma and fear out of rainstorms. If your toddler's fear is intense, have pretend lightning and thunderstorm parties. You can buy a small strobe light and purchase thunderstorm sounds. You can have special treats and play rain games during your pretend thunderstorm. When there is a real thunderstorm you can re-create a similar party with treats and games. This helps your toddler make a positive association with the sounds of a storm.

Bedtime rituals

In order for toddlers to feel more in control at night, they develop rigid bedtime routines that can quickly evolve into rituals. What is the difference between a routine and a ritual? A routine is comforting, but the child is flexible if the routine doesn't go as planned. A ritual has to be done in exactly the same way each time. If a ritual is not done, the toddler will have heightened anxiety and panic.

Anxious toddlers exhibit many rigid and ritualistic behaviors throughout the day, but bedtime by far has the most rituals. Bedtime brings up many insecurities for young children, which increases their desire to establish comforting rituals. Parents are also more likely to have a predictable routine at night that can inadvertently cater to ritualistic behavior.

Having an order to bedtime is helpful and comforting. Taking a bath, reading a book, getting tucked in are all predictable routines for a toddler. When your toddler starts requiring you to do things in a certain way or for a certain number of times, you've moved from routine to ritual. The hard part is delineating what is routine and what is ritualistic behavior. Keeping things in a particular order is a routine and can be comforting. Reading a certain number of books or saying good night to various things in the room are also routine-oriented behaviors. If your toddler wants to line up their stuffed animals in a certain way, that is usually more ritualistic behavior. If they do not want any wrinkles on their bed or they require you to say an *exact* phrase when you leave (like "I love you too")—those are more likely to be ritualistic behaviors. If your toddler has routines, the routines will not expand, but if your toddler has rituals, they will continue to grow and be more demanding.

You can help your child by slowly teaching them to be more adaptable. As we discussed in the first chapter, you have to assess your toddler's ability to handle challenges and change. If your toddler had a long, difficult day, don't choose that night to teach them to be more flexible. If your toddler likes their stuffed animals set up in a certain way, try to get them to set them up in a different way. If they don't want any wrinkles on their bed, explain to them that wrinkles are alright and that you sleep with wrinkles on your bed. If they insist that you smooth out their wrinkles, have them do it themselves. Removing yourself from your toddler's rituals is the first step to change. You can respond to them by saying something like, "If you don't want wrinkles then you can smooth out your own blanket. Mommy thinks wrinkles are okay."

If your child wants you to come back into their room to hug them repeatedly or wants you to say, "I love you too" over and over again, you are completing the loop for your child's ritual. It is hard for parents to deny their child another hug or to stop saying, "I love you too," but this behavior is anxiety based and the more you contribute to the behavior, the more you are enabling the ritual. One way to stop the loop would go something like this:

Child: I love you.

Parent: Love you!

Child: No, you say—I love you too!

Parent: Love ya!

Child: Nooo! You say—I love you too!

Parent: You don't control how I talk. You control your words and I control mine.

When you do not say or do things exactly as your toddler wants them, you are teaching them to be more flexible. You are also teaching them that they cannot control other people. This will be a valuable lesson as they get older, especially at school and with their peers.

Separation anxiety

Some toddlers have had no prior sleep issues and then suddenly they develop a fear of being left alone in their room. This can catch parents off guard as the behavior seems to come out of nowhere. Separation anxiety can be intense and can really disrupt bedtime. Toddlers are going through many developmental changes, and separation anxiety can occur throughout these early stages of growth.

Your knee-jerk reaction will be to lie down with your toddler until they fall asleep or to let them fall asleep in your bedroom. This quickly takes care of your toddler's fears and gets you to bed that much quicker. The downfall to this approach is the habit you will be forming moving forward. As we discussed earlier in this chapter, anxious children will not spontaneously decide they should sleep on their own. If you don't have a problem lying down with your child or having them sleep in your bedroom for the remainder of their time at home, then this is not a concern. If you want your child to sleep independently at some point, you don't want to start encouraging this habit.

If your child is attached to a blanket or a stuffed animal, these items are usually called transitional objects. These attachments help them feel safe when you are not with them. If they have a transitional object, make sure they have it when they are going to sleep. If they are not attached to an object or blanket, you might want to try and incorporate one into their bedtime routine.

When putting your child to bed, keep the routine that you had prior to them developing separation anxiety. It will be tempting to alter your routine to fix the problem quickly, but try to stay strong. If your routine ends with patting or rubbing your child, you might want to end with a more definitive ending, such as singing three songs or giving two kisses, which gives your child an indication and warning of when you are leaving. If you end by rubbing their head, they will cry and ask you to stay longer. When you end with three songs, you can count on your hand as you sing each song giving them a visual indicator of when tuck-in will be over.

When you leave the room, your toddler will probably start screaming or coming to the door (if they aren't in a crib). If your toddler is in a bed and they don't have great dexterity yet, you can put up a baby gate to keep them in their room. If you can't use a gate, sit in the hall out of their view. If they come out, put them back to bed with a quick reassurance such as, "Go to bed. You are alright." If they are not coming out, but they are still screaming, go in every five minutes to comfort them. It is best to be robotic and simplistic with what you say such as, "Lie down. You are alright." Refrain from over-processing with your child. You can space out the time between "resetting" your child depending on their level of panic. I have worked with children who get so worked up they gag and throw up. If you go in every five minutes, your child usually does not have time to escalate to that level. This process will seem tedious and torturous, but it is well worth the pain. Without going through these steps, your child is much more likely to have long-term sleep problems.

Sleep disturbances

As a toddler's imagination grows, so does the likelihood that they may start having bad dreams. The world can be scary for a toddler and they are taking in new things on a daily basis.

Their brain has to process this information and it often comes in the form of nightmares. Nightmares are perfectly normal and are not usually a sign of a bigger problem. Anxious toddlers tend to have more nightmares than the average toddler because they have more fears and phobias.

When your child wakes up from a bad dream, they might be screaming or crying. It is helpful to try and wake them up fully in order to pull them completely out of their dream state. Tell your child it was just a dream and that they are alright. They may not get the concept of what a dream is at this point, but it is helpful to start labeling it. In order to "reset" your toddler, you want to get their mind on something else. If you just reassure them that they are alright and they fall back to sleep, it is likely they will go back to dreaming about the same topic. Try to get your toddler into a conversation. You can discuss something fun that they are going to do the next day or you can tell them a happy story. Once they have focused on another topic or story, you can try and soothe them back to sleep.

As a relaxation and distraction technique I will often have parents create a "world" with their child. This is something you can do with your child at bedtime. Start by asking your child what type of world they would like to create. I have had children make candy lands, LEGO® worlds and puppy worlds—whatever they love! Help start the process by asking them to describe what their world looks like, who lives there and what are the smells and sounds in the world. The more elements they can imagine, the more real the world will become. You don't want the world to have a story line because you are trying to relax the mind, not activate it. Although you are not encouraging a story line, your child can create fun things they can do in their world. Children can eat the candy trees, build with LEGO or groom the puppies. Monotonous activities will help your child relax and fall asleep quicker. You can end your tuck-in with them talking about their world. When you leave, you can tell your child to continue to think about their world until they fall asleep. If your child wakes up with a nightmare, you can "reset" them by telling them to think of their world. Once a child has a solid idea of what their world looks like, you can use this as a distraction technique even during the day when they are scared or upset about something.

If your child has frequent nightmares, you can use aromatherapy to encourage happier thoughts and dreams. Similar to how we talked about using it with monsters, tell your toddler the spray gives them "happy dreams." Lavender spray can promote a feeling of well-being and can encourage nicer dreams. There are also relaxation and guided imagery CDs that are especially designed for young children. If your child is anxious going to sleep and has bad dreams often, this is a positive, uplifting way to move them into a sleep state.

Night terrors are different from bad dreams in that they are a partial arousal from non-REM sleep. REM (rapid eye movement) sleep is one of the deepest stages of our sleep cycle and is where we usually have our most lucid dreams. If your child suddenly wakes up with a blood-curdling scream, heart pounding, and dripping in sweat, incoherent and inconsolable, it might be a night terror. Children who are having night terrors are not fully awake and can be aggressive and remain inconsolable for an extended period of time. Night terrors are a physiological issue, similar to sleep walking, and children do not have memories of a nightmare associated with them. They usually happen in the initial hours of sleep. Night terrors can occur with a higher frequency if your child is over tired or has a poor diet, but those issues alone do not cause night terrors. Night terrors can run in families who have a history of sleep disorders or sleep disturbances. It is best to not wake up your child when they are having a night terror. Comfort them and make sure they are safe, while protecting yourself from their thrashing limbs until they fall back to sleep. If you suspect your child is having night terrors, describe the situation to a pediatrician. Children usually grow out of night terrors and need no further treatment. If night terrors become a household disruption, track what time your child usually wakes up with one. Once you see a pattern, wake your child up 15–30 minutes before that time to take them to the bathroom. This can "reset" your child and disrupt their sleep cycle, preventing the night terror. If you are going to try scheduled awakenings, it is important to put your child to bed at the same time each night. Most children grow out of having night terrors and they are not indicative of anxiety or trauma in themselves.

Staying in bed

In general, anxious toddlers are not good sleepers. They have a hard time getting to sleep and staying asleep. Some parents feel as if they still have a newborn at home! These toddlers wake up frequently throughout the night and are very early risers! They are light sleepers, usually because they are hypervigilant and are subconsciously scanning the environment for unfamiliar sounds and noises.

If your child is not a climber, it is better to try and keep them in a crib for as long as you can. This helps them feel secure and it also buys you time until your toddler is a little more emotionally mature and can handle the additional freedom. If your child does not have the dexterity to open a baby gate (and there are some very hard baby gates), keep one on their door frame until they are able to accept the boundaries of staying in their room. When you feel they are ready, keep the gate open but do not remove it from their door.

Some parents I have worked with have missed the signs of anxiety at night. Their child finds every excuse to come out of bed and parents often think their child is just stalling. Yes, they *are* stalling—but why? Older toddlers will tell me they don't want to go to bed until everyone else goes to bed. They are anxious they might be missing something if they are asleep and everyone else is awake. Other toddlers are just the opposite. They want their parents to stay up and "stand guard" over them and they are fearful that their parents will go to bed and leave them unprotected. These toddlers often come out to check on their parents and get reassurance that everything is alright.

The first step in getting your child to stay in bed is to address *all* their needs before you tuck them it. Do they need a drink? Do they need to go to the bathroom? Depending on whether or not the child has a bedwetting issue or is still in pull-ups, some parents will leave a cup of water by the side of their bed. This eliminates the "I neeeeed a drink!" demand. Make your child go to the bathroom before you put them to bed. This eliminates the "I have to go potty!" demand!

Be stern, and set up consequences if your child gets out of bed. If your child still has a baby gate, you can tell them, "If you get up again, I am going to close your baby gate." If you don't have a baby gate you can have a "stay-in-bed treasure box" where they earn a prize the next morning for staying in bed. Conversely, you can take away a privilege for the next morning. Give your child three strikes—a strike each time they get out of bed. This helps teach them the appropriate behavior and gives them time to correct their behavior before they bear the consequences.

If you have a camera in your child's room to help them feel safe, it can also be used to maintain boundaries and to ensure they don't get out of bed. When you see your child getting out of bed, you can catch them before they reach the door and tell them through the camera to get back in bed. This tends to eliminate that behavior quickly, as they never know when you are actually watching them.

Some toddlers wake up at 4am and are ready to start their day! For the early risers, a wonderful toddler clock has been created! Among the various products that help toddlers become aware of time (you can find them online and on Amazon), there

89

are clocks that you can program to turn green at a certain time to alert the toddler to the fact that it is morning and they can leave their room. It takes time for toddlers to adapt to this process and it isn't instantly effective. Older toddlers will get this concept quicker and will be more likely to adhere to the rules of "green clock" awakening. You can tell your toddler, "When your clock is green you can wake up and leave your room. If your clock isn't green, it isn't morning time yet and you shouldn't leave your room because everyone is still sleeping."

Toddlers who are light sleepers have no concept of time and can wake up at 4am and think that it is early morning. The green clock helps to signal to those toddlers what time to wake up. If your child wakes up early, you can tell them that their clock isn't green and that they need to go back to bed. This clock isn't a miracle worker and it will still take some effort to keep your child in their bed and in their room. The addition of a gate (if your child can't open one) is a perfect interim solution until your toddler is old enough to understand and respect boundaries and rules more effectively.

• • • • • • • • • • • • • •

CHAPTER 5

Bathroom Battles

Carol and Jim

Carol and Jim had little trouble potty training their first child Garrett. That is why they were surprised at the struggles they faced with Emma. Emma was so different from Garrett on every level. Garrett was an easygoing child, quick to adapt and learn new things. Emma struggled with changes and had a hard time with loud noises and fears.

Initially, Emma seemed to get the concept of potty training rather quickly. She sat on her small portable potty and peed without issue. They didn't even have to use sticker charts or candy as a reward, like they had with Garrett! Carol thought potty training was going to be easy! Once Emma seemed to master the portable potty, they bought a small ring to go on top of the toilet and moved toileting to the bathroom. They bought a small stool that Emma could use to climb up onto the toilet. The ring allowed her to sit on top of the toilet without falling in.

Emma refused to go poop on the toilet. She didn't seem to have trouble peeing in the toilet, but for some reason she would not poop! Emma would go around holding her bottom and would cry out in pain. Her parents would encourage her to go to the bathroom, but Emma refused. Initially, Carol was told by her pediatrician and her close friends that she should be patient and that Emma would catch on, like all kids do. Carol tried to not get into battles with Emma.

Emma still wore pull-ups to bed and Jim noticed that whenever he put Emma's pull-up on at night, she immediately pooped in her diaper. This would upset him and he'd ask her, "Why did you wait until I put a pull-up on you? I just asked you if you had to go to the bathroom and you said no!" No matter how many times Jim would have her sit on the toilet prior to bedtime, Emma would poop as soon as she was in her diaper.

Emma started having a hard time pooping, even when she was in a diaper. When Jim tried to get her ready for bed, he'd frequently find her hiding in the corner of her room, face bright red and sweaty, struggling to poop. She would start to cry and it would take her forever to poop. When Jim changed her diaper he'd find just small, hard balls of feces.

Emma started complaining about her tummy hurting and Carol started to get concerned. Emma would cry throughout the day saying, "Tummy hurt. Tummy hurt." Finally, Carol took Emma to the doctor. The doctor felt her stomach and determined that she was very constipated. The doctor gave her medicine to help clear her out and recommended that she stay on a stool softener and eat a high fiber diet. Carol thought it was hard enough to get Emma to eat, let alone eat a high fiber diet!

Although Emma's pain went away, her behavior around toileting didn't change. She continued to hold her bottom throughout the day and would say she didn't have to go when asked. Carol was concerned and didn't want her to get constipated again, so she started putting pull-ups on her when she thought she might have to go poop. Like clockwork, Emma would run off to a corner of the room or behind the couch and strain as she tried to poop.

When Emma was out in public, toileting was even worse. Emma would refuse to go to the toilet in public restrooms. She would kick and scream and would refuse to go into the room. Her mom did not know what to do. The automatic flusher scared Emma and she grew fearful that all public restrooms had them.

When she was at a friend's house she was slightly better, but her mom had to coax her to go to the toilet.

Even when Emma had to pee, she started to need her mom to come into the bathroom with her. She would refuse to go anywhere near the bathroom, unless her mom would walk in with her. Emma didn't want to flush the toilet and she would run out before her mom flushed it for her. She also got nervous sitting on the toilet and would often hold onto the sides of the seat with a tight grip.

Carol started to become frustrated and was at a loss as to what to do. She was told by one of her friends that Emma was just being stubborn and that she should just sit her on the toilet until she went. Carol tried that and it didn't go too well. Emma started screaming with panic and Carol took some of her TV time away. Jim told Carol that maybe they should just back off and that Emma would eventually come around.

Later that year when Carol and Jim wanted to put Emma into pre-school with all her friends, they were told that unless she was fully toilet trained she could not enroll. They were devastated and didn't know what to do.

Emma

Emma didn't like change. So when her mom and dad took her diaper off and had her sit on this small plastic toilet, she didn't know what to think. It took a little while to figure out what her mom and dad were wanting her to do. She had seen her parents and brother go on the big toilet before and she knew they didn't wear diapers. She started to like the feeling of controlling her pee and did not like being wet. Her mom and dad seemed pleased and they would cheer and clap every time she went to the bathroom. She never pooped in her small potty. Poop was for diapers.

Then for some reason her mom took her plastic potty away and wanted her to go into the bathroom. The huge toilet had a small ring on it and there were steps for her to use to reach the top. It was scary at the top and she felt as if she might fall over. She held onto the sides, but she was worried about falling into the toilet. What if she fell in? Would she get swallowed up by the black hole at the bottom? Where did the poop go after it was flushed away? Would that happen to her?

When her mom flushed the toilet it was so loud. She would try and run out of the room before her mom flushed the toilet. The noise scared her and hurt her ears. She especially didn't like the loud flush of toilets when they were out. Sometimes the toilet would flush while she was still on it! That was the scariest thing of all. The noise was ten times louder than at home and for some reason there were no handles to flush the toilets. The toilet decided to flush on its own and she never knew when that would be! She decided to never go to the toilet in those scary bathrooms again.

At bedtime her dad would put her in a pull-up. Finally! She would rush to the corner of her room so no one could see her and she would go poop. She was confused about why her dad would yell at her afterwards? He was the one who put her in a diaper. Diapers are for pooping. Eventually she tried to not poop at all. She was scared of pooping on the toilet and her dad got so mad when she pooped in a diaper. Her tummy often hurt. Her mom said it was because she needed to poop. She didn't feel as if she had to go.

Her parents didn't seem happy with her anymore. They didn't cheer when she peed and they started sitting her on the toilet and not letting her get off until she pooped. She didn't feel as if she had to poop—even if she had wanted to go. Her mom took away TV time, but Emma still didn't feel as if she had to go to the bathroom. She cried. Her mom seemed frustrated.

She soon got scared of even going into the bathroom. It was dark and her mom might make her sit there for a long time. It had started to really hurt when she tried to go poop and one time it took her a long time to get it all out. If her mom asked her if she needed to go to the toilet she'd quickly say no. She didn't want the pain. She didn't want her mom to yell at her. She *didn't want to be forced to sit there for what felt like forever! Her parents told her that she wouldn't be able to go to school like the rest of her big girl friends. She was sad. Oh well, I guess I can't go to school. Whatever that means!*

Fears

Toileting can trigger many fears in the anxious toddler. Although many toddlers won't verbalize or aren't capable of verbalizing their fears, most toileting issues stem from them. Some toddlers are afraid of falling into the toilet. Although to us, this does not make any rational sense, the toddler's ability to understand spatial concepts is not fully developed. Their fear of falling into the toilet and being flushed away is a very real fear. They see other things disappear down the toilet—why can't it happen to them? Some toddlers even explore this weird phenomenon by taking random items and seeing if they can be flushed down the toilet as well. Sadly for their parents, the answer is usually yes!

Another common fear is the fear of bugs or snakes coming out of the toilet. If things can disappear down the hole, why can't things appear *from* the hole? This makes sense to the toddler who may have seen bugs coming up through the drains in the sink or the bathtub or has seen bugs in the bathroom itself. They are worried something is going to pop out of the water while they are sitting on the toilet.

If your toddler has ever witnessed the toilet overflowing, that might add to their toileting fears. The scene of having water and feces uncontrollably overflowing out of a toilet is a traumatizing one for the anxious toddler. They are worried about this happening when they are on the toilet. How can anyone guarantee that it won't happen again? Many toddlers won't flush because they have made the connection between flushing and the toilet overflowing.

••••••
95

Sometimes it is not the toilet your toddler is afraid of, but the bathroom itself. The bathroom is often dark and tends to separate parents from children. Parents will disappear into the bathroom and not let their toddler go with them. Anxious toddlers will often sit by the door crying, waiting for their parent to come out. Now their parent wants them to go in there…alone?!

The fear of germs usually doesn't start until a child is a little bit older, but the idea of getting "dirty" is very much a toddler fear. Some anxious toddlers don't like to get their hands dirty and the idea of getting poop on their hands is terrifying. These toddlers will refuse to wipe their bottoms and may go as far as avoiding the bathroom all together if it means they might have to wipe. These children also have a fear of flushing because they are afraid the water and poop will splash up and get them wet and dirty.

If your toddler is afraid of germs at this stage of development, it is probably from someone inadvertently modeling that behavior. If your child is told, "Don't touch the seat, it has germs" and "Wash your hands really well after you go to the toilet because you have germs on your hands," your anxious toddler might develop an early fear of germs. As children get older and are exposed to the knowledge of germs, they can develop these fears independent of someone else's beliefs.

Another less common toddler fear is the fear of flushing their poop away. Some toddlers are afraid to lose a part of themselves. This can sound very weird to those of you who don't have children with this issue, but it is a very real problem for some toddlers. Think of it as a precursor to hoarding behavior. Some children don't like to let go of anything—not their old toys, their old clothes or even your old couch. They save everything and get very upset when anything in their home changes or is replaced. These children also have a hard time losing things from their bodies, including hair, nails and yes—even poop. This can be so distressing to a toddler that they will, at times, refuse to poop all together.

So, if it is fear-based avoidance, how do you get your child to go to the bathroom? Most of these fears primarily affect defecating and are less likely to affect urinating. Some children have told me it's because they can pee quickly and get out of the bathroom. They are not sitting on the toilet for nearly as long and they are able to pee immediately, without having to wait or work at it. It is important to find out the origin of the fear. Although the end behavior is the same—withholding and avoiding pooping—the trigger is different for each child and that discovery is key to helping them move on.

Let's go through each fear one by one and discuss approaches for how you could help your toddler overcome them.

Fear of falling in

If your child is afraid they will fall into the toilet, explain to them that they are too big to fall in and that if they did, they would just get wet. Blow a balloon up halfway and place it in the toilet. Ask your toddler if they are bigger or smaller than the balloon. Then flush the toilet with the balloon still in it. Have your toddler watch as the balloon doesn't get sucked down into the black hole. Explain to them that even the balloon, which is much much smaller than them, was too big to go through the black hole and disappear. Having a secure toddler ring with handles and a step stool that brings them comfortably up to the top of the toilet can improve their feeling of security as well.

Fear of bugs and snakes

Talk to your child about bugs in the water. Can most bugs survive in water? Yes, some, but not most—remember this isn't a lesson in entomology. Discuss with them how bugs don't swim and can't come up into the toilet through the water. Even though this isn't completely true of snakes, it's not the time to have a completely frank conversation about this. If your child has seen bugs in the bathroom or has seen bugs coming out of the drain, explain to them that the drain was dry and that they did not go through water to come out of the drain. If you do have a bug problem in your bathroom, it might be a good idea to spray in there when your child is not around to prevent further bug encounters.

Fear of the toilet overflowing

Children who are afraid of the toilet overflowing are usually the most concerned with flushing. Have your child repeatedly flush the toilet. Talk to them about how the toilet doesn't usually overflow. If they are reluctant to flush the toilet, start with them watching you flush it. If this is too overwhelming for them, have them stand right outside the door while you flush the toilet. Work your way up to having them repeatedly flushing the toilet themselves. *Desensitizing* is an approach we will use over and over again in this book. To desensitize, you slowly expose your child to their fear in order to help them adapt and overcome it. To make your child more receptive to desensitizing approaches, you can tell your child that if they do this "challenge" they will earn a treasure box reward. Once your child is able to flush repeatedly without anxiety, take colored ice cubes (made with food coloring) and throw them in the toilet. Have your toddler repeatedly flush with the colored ice cubes. The ice cubes represent the poop and the irrational belief that the toilet won't flush if there is something actually in it.

Fear of the bathroom

If your toddler is withholding their poop because they don't want to go to the bathroom alone, it is *more* important that they poop regularly than that they go alone. Go to the bathroom with your toddler until they are no longer withholding their poop. Once you have a good routine and your toddler is no longer getting constipated, you can start working on getting them to go to the toilet independently. You can set up challenges with your toddler. When they ask for you to go to the bathroom with them, ask if they want to take a challenge. Tell them they can earn a prize if they go to the bathroom all by themselves. This will encourage your toddler to be more independent and to face their fears.

Fear of getting dirty

If your toddler is afraid of getting their hands dirty, they are probably exhibiting these types of behaviors outside the bathroom as well. You can work on this issue outside the bathroom, as well as inside. Encourage messy play by setting up chocolate pudding finger painting and other messy play activities. Talk to your child and tell them that it is alright if they get dirty, that they can wash their hands. In the bathroom, encourage independent wiping. You can tell them that they need to at least do the first wipe and then you can help them. It is normal for toddlers to need help wiping at this stage of development, but you don't want it to be fear based. Encourage challenges if they wipe without your help and reward them with a prize from the treasure box.

Fear of losing a part of themselves

As strange as this problem may sound, some toddlers have a very real fear of letting go of their poop. This issue is bigger than just the fear of losing their poop. These children have a hard time letting go of anything. You can help your child by helping them let go of things outside the bathroom. Many parents will acquiesce to their child's needs to hold onto nonsensical items they gather throughout their day. This isn't a major issue unless it is impeding their development. If they are having toileting issues due to this issue, it has become a problem that needs to be addressed. Have your child periodically go through their things and let one item go.

Explain to them that they do not need it anymore. If they feel bad throwing their stuff away, you can explain how donating their stuff works.

When it comes to poop, explain to your child the purpose of poop. Tell your child that their food goes through them and their body takes all the good things out of their food. The poop is the *garbage* that their body doesn't want and so it is being discarded. It is important to take the *garbage* out by going poop because you don't want to have all this garbage in your body. If they have been withholding their poop due to this fear, you might want to start with flushing the poop for them after they leave the bathroom. The next step would be for them to flush their poop themselves. It might help them if they close the lid before they flush. As always, challenges and treasure box rewards are always helpful and facilitate change more quickly.

Control

Some children have issues around the bathroom because they feel as if they have no control over other areas of their lives. If you and your child get into control battles often, this may be their way of expressing their desire for control. You can help your child feel as if they are more in control by taking a step back from their toilet training. Remove yourself from the toileting battle by pretending to be indifferent to their toileting success. I know this can be very hard to do, especially with the mess and frustration that comes along with toilet training. Your child may have been feeding off your reactions whether positive or negative and responding accordingly. Set up a treasure box for successfully going to the bathroom. Have your child pick out their prizes so they are fully engaged in the process. Tell them where the treasure box is (put it up high) and let them know that if they go to the toilet you will get the treasure box down for them. If your child has accidents, avoid any verbal exchange and silently clean up the mess. If your child successfully goes to the toilet, give your child the treasure box with a neutral response such as, "You went to the toilet, so you get a treasure box prize." With this approach the focus becomes more on the toilet and the treasure box and less on meeting or not meeting your expectations.

Sensory issues

Some toileting problems have more to do with sensory issues. Some children will take their poop and smear it on the walls. This can be very alarming and upsetting for parents. For some of these children, they are seeking sensory input, for others it might be behavioral. We will discuss those that who seeking sensory input, as that tends to be the cause for anxious children. These children like the feel of mushy warm poop, as gross as that seems to us! Some toddlers are not bothered by the idea of touching poop and to them it is another curious thing in their environment for them to explore. This is especially true for younger toddlers. To help discourage this behavior, have finger paint in the bathroom. Let your child know (if they have touched their poop in the past) that it is not okay to touch poop, but they can use finger paint in the bathtub. You can lightly warm up the paint to give your child the same physical sensation as their poop. Praise your child for asking to use the finger paint instead of smearing the poop on the walls. If you are a relaxed parent, you can have your child paint in the bathtub with or without their clothes on after they go poop, as a reward.

Some toddlers have the opposite problem and they avoid sensory input. They do not like the feel of their hands getting wet and therefore don't want to go to the bathroom. They do not want to wash their hands and will often tell their parents that they didn't touch anything so they don't have to wash their hands. You can help your child get used to the feeling of wet hands by having them wash their hands at the kitchen sink. You can also use antibacterial gel that doesn't require water after they go to the bathroom.

Pain avoidance

Anxious toddlers tend to have good memories. This will help them throughout much of life, but will also be a disadvantage on another level. Traumatic experiences are filed away for easy recall and for future avoidance. This is true for bad food experiences, bad friend experiences and bad poop experiences! If your child is refusing to go poop and you don't know why, you might start with looking at their pooping history. Were they constipated as infants? Have they had painful experiences defecating? If so, this may be the cause of their reluctance to poop more frequently. Unfortunately, this problem becomes a vicious cycle, as further withholding will cause more constipation and pain. Talk with your pediatrician about what they would recommend to help soften your child's stools and make them less painful. If it is an ongoing problem you can use over-the-counter fiber gummies to keep your child regular.

CHAPTER 6

• • • • • • • • • • • • • •

Bath Time Fights

Tami and Rick

Tami and Rick have two children, Hayden, aged three, and Jackson, aged five. The couple has a good system of sharing responsibilities and delineating tasks. Rick is on bath time duty as Tami cleans up after dinner. In the past Rick really enjoyed his bath time with the kids. He felt that bath time was a relaxing time where he got to bond with the boys before they had to go to bed. Lately Rick would do anything to trade jobs with Tami.

About a month ago, Rick's three-year-old son Hayden developed a fear of the bath. Rick wasn't able to pinpoint the cause of Hayden's new fear. One night Hayden started running around when it was bath time. Rick tried to settle him down, but Hayden was full of energy. Finally, when Rick started the bath water, Hayden started screaming, "No bath! No bath!" Rick didn't think it was that big a deal, until Hayden refused to take off his clothes. After an hour-long struggle, Rick realized they had a big problem on their hands!

It seemed as if out of the blue had Hayden started refusing to take a bath. Tami reminded Rick how it had been hard to get Hayden to take a bath or get him into the pool when he was a baby. They laughed about how he would just stand in the bath and refuse to sit down. They would quickly wash his body and his hair and then take him out of the bathtub. Hayden hadn't liked getting fully into the water and he didn't like getting his hair washed, but he had got over those fears. Thankfully, bath time became another playtime and he and his brother Jackson would stay in there for hours if they could. So why the sudden new fear?

Rick tried to talk to Hayden about why he didn't like taking a bath, but he wouldn't say. Rick added new, fun toys, but nothing enticed Hayden to get back into the water. Rick started giving the boys separate baths because he felt bad for Jackson and didn't want him to have to be around for Hayden's bath-time meltdowns. Now he spent what seemed like hours on bath time. What was once a quick 30-minute job had turned into a few hours of torture!

After bathing Jackson, Rick would have Tami tuck him in as he took on the task of bathing Hayden. He would get the water ready and then take a screaming Hayden and place him in the bath. Hayden would yell and try to get out of the bath. Rick would try to quickly soap him up and wash his hair, as Hayden would try and claw his way out of the tub. Bath time left its marks both physically and emotionally each night. Rick thought this wasn't what he signed up for when he agreed to do bath time. Where had his bonding time gone?

One night before Rick was about to put Hayden into his bath, he started to scream, "Nooo! Bug! Bug!" as he pointed to a very small black dot floating under the water. Rick explained to Hayden that the black dot wasn't a bug, but a speck of dirt floating in the water. The dot was so small it was hard for Rick even to fish it out of the bath—but he eventually did. "See," he told Hayden, "dirt is all gone." Hayden still cried when he was put into the bath, but he didn't claw his way out of the tub that evening.

Rick and Tami talked and thought maybe he was afraid that bugs were in the bath. Was he afraid of bugs when they went outside in the backyard? Rick decided to put bubbles in the bath to see if that would help Hayden not panic about every black speck he saw. Rick prepared himself for his nightly battle as he explained to Hayden that he was going to make his bath all bubbly. When Rick lifted Hayden into the tub he was shocked by the silence. Why wasn't Hayden screaming? He looked over and saw Hayden blowing some of the bubbles and placing them on his chin for a beard. "Look daddy, I got beard like you!" Hayden's giggles could be heard down the hall. Tami peered into the bathroom with awe, "What have we here? A happy boy?" Rick put his fingers to his lips, as he didn't want anything to break this moment of peace.

Hayden

Hayden never liked water. When he was a baby the water felt too hot. His legs and body felt weird under the water. The water would splash up and gather around his stomach. He didn't like that feeling, so he always stood up. When his dad would put yellow bubbly stuff on his hair it would pour down his face. One time it got in his eyes and his eyes burned. Ouch! He did not like that yellow bubbly stuff and when he saw the bottle he would start to scream. Soon they put him in the bath with his brother. His brother was so much fun that he forgot all about the scary water and the yellow bubbly stuff.

One day when his dad was giving him and his brother a bath, he saw a black bug moving towards his leg. It went by so fast he really wasn't able to fully see what it was, but he had seen black bugs in their backyard. He yelped and stood up. He told his dad, "Out! I am all done!" and his dad pulled him from the bath remarking, "That was a quick one!"

The next night he was scared of going into the bathtub again. What if that big scary black bug is back? It might try to bite me? Eat me? Yikes! His dad yelled, "Two minutes before you have to take a bath boys." He didn't want a bath and he didn't know what to do. All he could think of was that big black bug that almost ate him the night before. He started to run around. His dad told him to calm down, but he couldn't! When his dad tried *to take his clothes off he screamed as if his life depended on it. Why would his dad want to put him in a bath full of black bugs?*

He decided baths were not for him and that he was not going to go into one easily. He noticed Jackson didn't take a bath with him anymore and he wondered if Jackson was scared of the black bugs too. No matter how hard he cried, his dad continued to lift him up and put him in the bath. He thought he saw a black bug when his legs hit the water and he clawed at his dad's arms trying to get him to pull him out of the tub.

One day he thought he saw a black bug before his dad lifted him up into the bath. He screamed, "Bug! Bug!" so his dad would see them too. He expected his dad to get scared and to acknowledge the black bugs too, but all he said was "That's not a bug. That's dirt." Dirt? Could it be dirt? Is dirt black? He thought dirt was brown. Why was a speck of dirt in his bathtub? He was so busy thinking about this that his bath was over before he knew it.

The next night his dad told him he was going to take a bubble bath. Oh no, not the yellow bubbly stuff that burned his eyes. Could bath time get any worse? But then he saw his bath had transformed into a winter wonderland of bubble snow. White fluff oozed out of the bathtub and he couldn't even see the bottom of the tub! He was excited to play with the bubbles. He blew at them. He thought these bubbles would make a great beard! He looked at his reflection through the metal water facet. He started to laugh! "I look like my dad with a beard," he declared!

Fears

Although most parents will report that their toddlers love taking baths, the anxious toddler can have some serious struggles around bath time. Toddlers can refuse to take baths for many different reasons; however, the end result is usually the same—a screaming, red-faced toddler with a death grip, determined to not get into the tub.

Some toddlers may not exhibit overt fears getting into the bath. If your toddler refuses to sit in their bath, this may be an indication that they are having some anxiety. Toddlers with fears or sensory issues prefer to stand in the water to have more control. Other toddlers start to have avoidant, hyperactive behavior before bath time. They will run around and try to avoid taking a bath. Parents can misinterpret this behavior as defiance and can get even sterner. If your child is not usually hyperactive or defiant, pay attention to when your child *is* exhibiting these behaviors, as it might be a sign of anxiety.

It is important to get to the heart of the fear in order to accurately address it. Talk with your child about why they don't like taking baths. Observe their reactions and see when their fear response kicks in. Do they get scared when you pull up the drain? Are they nervous to get in? Do they panic when it is time to wash their hair? Many parents are stumped about what is causing their toddler's fears. The most common bath time fears are discussed below.

Fear of the drain

Toddlers, even those who do not have anxiety, are commonly afraid of the dreaded drain. Like the toilet fear, toddlers are afraid they might go down the drain. As ludicrous as this sounds to us, this is a very real fear for them. As we discussed earlier, toddler's spatial abilities are just developing and they do not have the cognitive capacity to recognize that they will not fit down the drain. They see the water swirl around and disappear, sucking toys in its direction. Often the drain will make a loud gurgling sound as it aggressively swallows the rest of the bath water. For the sensitive child, this can be scary and make them want to avoid taking a bath altogether.

If you are not sure if this might be your child's fear, observe them when you drain the bath. Do they claw to get out of the tub when you pull the drain? Do they scoot to the other side of the bath? Do they fearfully pull their toys closer to them as the water drains? If this seems to be the case, there are several things you can do to help your toddler. Like you did for the toilet fear, put a small balloon in the tub and show them how it does not go down the drain. Put the balloon up to them and show them how much bigger they are than the balloon. Another option is to have them get out of the bath before you drain the tub. If they are fearful of the sounds associated with draining the tub, you can have them leave the bathroom before you unplug the drain. Eventually though, it is good to have your child acclimatize to the drain and the sounds of bath time. You don't want to enable your child's fears permanently by helping them avoid them. Having your child bathed is more important than having them get used to the drain. Once they are comfortable taking baths again, you can slowly integrate them back into the bathroom and eventually into the tub when you are draining the water.

Fear of bugs coming out of the drain

Yes, another drain issue. Some children are not afraid of falling into the drain, but of things coming out of it. They worry that bugs are going to crawl or swim out of the drain. Most fears of the anxious toddler do not stem from actual experiences or trauma. Your toddler didn't have to see a bug crawl out of your bathtub to imagine the possibility. They may just imagine that a bug logically could come through the black, ominous drain that lurks in their tub. Like many toddler fears, their thoughts are not always rational. Although bugs can come through drains (which really doesn't help this cause!), the likelihood of a bug swimming through running water and making it up into the bathtub is very small.

If, like Hayden, from this chapter's vignette, your child is afraid of specks of dirt in their bath, they are probably afraid of bugs. As odd as this sounds, fearing that there are bugs in the bath is a common fear among anxious toddlers. This might take some acute observation to figure out, as toddlers may not be expressive about what scares them.

If your toddler is afraid of bugs, you can try bubble bath. Bubbles conceal all those tiny mysterious little specks of nothing that seem to drive anxious toddlers crazy. Bubbles can be a good deterrent for your child and can help them focus on having fun and prevent them from fixating on playing the I-spy-the-bug game.

However, some toddlers get freaked out by bubbles and have an equally terrifying response to bubbles as they do to bugs. Some children can find bubbles scary because they cannot see what may be lurking under the water. Unfortunately, this is a trial-and-error approach and you may not know how your toddler will feel until you actually try using bubbles. You can put some in the sink first and have them play with them if you want to be cautious and introduce the concept slowly.

Fear of wrinkles on the skin

Anxious toddlers do not like change and that goes for bodily changes as well. For most of us, watching our skin prune up like an old raisin as we sit in the tub is not a big deal. To the anxious toddler, wrinkled fingers are scary, confusing and mystifying. They worry, "What if my fingers stay this way? What if I get wrinkled all over?" To some children, this fear is so upsetting that they want to avoid water in its entirety. You many not even realize this is what your child is upset about. One possible way to tell is to look at how your child holds their hands after a bath. Toddlers who have this fear will often ball up their hands and keep them in tight fists as they come out of the tub. Some children also do this because of sensory issues, but we will discuss that in a later section.

An immediate fix, if you are concerned about bath avoidance, is to help your child learn to take a shower. Wrinkled fingers happen less often in the shower and with a quick shower it shouldn't happen at all. Eventually, however, you want to teach your child to face their fears and overcome them. You can slowly reintroduce your child to a bath and have them adapt to the changes to their fingers. You can point out that a few minutes afterwards their fingers turn back to normal. You can talk about how our body changes. You can use eating as an example. When you eat, your tummy gets big because it is full of food. After your tummy has taken all the food and used it for your body, your tummy gets smaller again. This helps your child link to another bodily change that is less scary and more relatable.

I pooped or peed in the bath!

Toddlers don't always have full control over their bowels and some toddlers accidentally pee or poop in the tub. This can surprise your child and make them feel as if they have no control. They may also feel concerned that the bathtub has had pee or poop in it. For some toddlers this type of incident may be enough for them to want to avoid taking baths.

If your child has had a toileting accident in the bath and is now avoiding baths, talk with them. Ask them if they are scared they might go to the toilet again in the tub. Reassure them that you washed the tub so it is nice and clean, and that accidents happen. Have your child go to the bathroom just before getting into the bath. Tell your child that they went to the toilet and got all their pee and poop out, so there shouldn't be any accidents.

Fear of slipping in the bath

Some toddlers have accidentally slipped in the tub and are now afraid to go back in. This can be especially frightening if they fell under the water. Sometimes getting new bath mats or fun, no-slip shower stickers in the shape of animals or other things can help to reassure them that something has been done about this problem.

Fear of bedtime

Sometimes it is not the bath at all, but rather what comes after the bath that is causing the anxiety. If your toddler runs around and seems to be avoiding the bath, but shows none of the fears above, there is a possibility that they are afraid of going to sleep. Bedtime fears can be so strong that even activities that are precursors to bedtime trigger anxiety and avoidance. If your child has major issues around sleep, bath time might not be the true problem. For this fear, it is better to focus on the origin of the fear—bedtime—rather than the symptom—bath time. To help differentiate the problem further, try giving your toddler a bath in the morning. If the bath-time struggles go away, it is most likely a bedtime issue.

Sensory fears

Bath time can trigger many sensory fears. We will cover sensory integration issues more fully in Chapter 11, but for now let's address how these manifest at bath time. Children with sensory issues can be more sensitive to sounds, feelings and smells around them. A bath can trigger many different sensory experiences. The temperature may seem fine to us, but to your child it is scalding. Once you put cold water in the bath to cool it down, the bath becomes too cold. This temperature issue can get tiring and frustrating.

For those children who are sensitive to temperature, it is best to put them in the bath as the water is still filling the tub. They can acclimatize to the temperature as the water is gathering around them and can let you know as the tub fills whether they want the water hotter or colder.

If your child is sensitive to sound, they may not like the sound of the water filling the tub. If your child is not sensitive to temperature, you can fill the tub before you bring them into the bathroom. This helps avoid the sensory overload they would feel if they were in the bathroom. If they are sensitive to both temperature and sound, you can give them swimmer's wax to put in their ears to help drown out the loud noise of the bath water.

Children with sensory issues have a hard time adjusting to how things feel on their body. This includes clothes, hugs and, yes, bath water. Most of us don't notice the feeling of water on our skin as we sit in the tub. We don't notice how some of our limbs are lighter or feel the subtle tickle of the water as it splashes up against our skin. Children with sensory issues notice and feel all of these changes and that can be overwhelming. Children who are just getting used to a bath may want to stand initially. It is alright to let your child stand and slowly adapt to the water. Parents will often say that their child never had problems with baths as a baby. This is probably true, but as we will discuss further in Chapter 11, struggles with sensory issues usually do not start showing up until toddlerhood.

Children with sensory issues are also more sensitive to getting water on their face. These children get overwhelmed when water is poured on their head or accidentally gets into their eyes, and that's just water—we haven't even talked about soap yet! One horrible incident of soap in their eyes can be enough for these children to avoid bath time altogether. A water visor is the best defense for this type of problem. If you have a hard time finding a bath water visor, you can search for one on the internet. They are also referred to as a baby bath visor or a shampoo visor and are pretty easy to find online. A bath visor helps your child feel more confident that water and soap will not accidentally get into their eyes.

Ironically, once you get your sensitive toddler into the tub, it is hard to get them out. That may seem confusing, but actually it makes a lot of sense. These children do not like change— change in temperature and change in physical sensations. Getting out of the tub can be a cold, drippy experience. Some children will actually ball up their hands so they can't feel the water dripping off them. Try keeping the bathroom as warm as possible and have their towel ready as soon as they come out of the tub.

Bath-time approaches

There are various approaches to help make bath time less stressful. Some things will work for your child and other will not. Approaches in general are a trial-and-error process. Below are ways to help make bath time more fun, thereby distracting your toddler from their anxiety and creating a more whimsical, fun atmosphere.

Colored bath

There is nothing more fun than choosing what color bath you would like! There are various products that add color to your child's bath without staining the tub. You can search for them online usually under "bath color tablets." Your child will find it fun to drop in two different colors and guess what color it will make the water. Some toddlers may be uncomfortable with their bath water changing color. For those toddlers, you may want to experiment in the sink first or use blue as your initial color.

Washcloth puppets

Washcloth puppets are fun and are usually easy to obtain. They encourage fantasy play and help distract your child from any potential fears. They also make scrubbing the body much more fun! When your child is afraid of getting water on their head, you can have the washcloth puppet pat them on their head during play, getting their hair wet.

Co-bathing

If your child has an acute fear of going into the tub and refuses to bathe at all, you might want to try getting into the bath with them. Your child will not get over their fears until they are able to re-integrate back into the bathtub. If they refuse to get into the tub, joining them may be your only option. Sometimes if you go into the tub first and play with their toys and bubbles, they may ask to join you. Other times it might involve you holding them and trying to soothe them as you enter the water.

Another option is to have your child bathe with a sibling close to their same age. Having a playmate in the bath can be a nice distraction and add to the excitement of the bath. Also, if they see that their big brother or big sister isn't afraid of the bath, maybe they will feel they shouldn't be either.

Dry washcloth

If your child hates to get water in their eyes, you can build their confidence by having a dry washcloth accessible right next to the tub. The quicker you can dry their little faces, the less trauma they will experience. With time you can teach your child to wipe their own face when they get overwhelmed. You always want to facilitate your child's independence and eventually have them take care of their own fears.

Fun baths

Fun baths are baths with themes—often done around the holidays. These baths are purely for fun and can be given in the middle of the day. They help solidify the idea that bath time can be a fun experience. A Christmas fun bath might have green water and foam Christmas trees that stick to the wall of the tub. You can add floating tinsel and hang candy canes around the bath taps. A Valentine's Day fun bath might have pink water and floating hearts. You can have edible, pink whipped cream paint and paint brushes for your child to paint on the walls.

Entertainment

It helps to have some activities in the tub to distract your little one from their fears. Anything foam will stick to the walls when wet. You can get foam letters, numbers or shapes for your child to play with while in the bath. You can also get bath crayons and bath finger paint for your child to create art. I would not crowd your tub with masses of toys, as that might overwhelm your child. Add one or two bath toys each bath time and rotate with new toys as you go.

Extended shower head

If you are having a really hard time getting your child into the tub, you might want to consider an extended shower head. Instead of a bath, have the extended shower head hanging down with the water pressure on low. Encourage your child to hold the shower head and control the water over their body. Handling the water directly will give your child a feeling of control and safety. You can eventually fill up the bath with some water and still have them use the shower head. This will get them slowly to adapt to a bath.

Mirror fun

Toddlers love mirrors. Having an unbreakable shower mirror can be a great distraction for your child. Stick the mirror as low down as possible, so your child can seen themselves without having to stand up. If they have bubbles, they can give themselves a beard or foamy hair. If they have soap crayons, they can paint their face and look at themselves in the mirror.

Ceiling fun

To help your child look up when shampooing their hair, stick something on the ceiling. You can hang up stars or pin a mobile to the ceiling and tell your child to look at them when you are washing their hair. This will help them look far enough up and will also encourage them to keep that position a little bit longer than they would otherwise. Any approach to making hair washing a success is worth trying.

Bubbles

Lots of people add bubble bath to their child's bath, but few people think to blow bubbles. This is a good option for kids who have sensitive skin that may be irritated by bubble bath, or for those who have a fear of bath bubbles. It is also a fun option to add to any bath. You can get clear plastic bubbles that do not disappear and will sit on top of the bath water until you actually pop them.

Water play

If your child has acute fears of the bath and won't go into the tub at all, you can try different environments to expose them to water. Have your child play in a small baby pool outside. You can add bubbles for further fun or throw a bar of soap into the pool to make it productive. Hose play is also a helpful way to give your child a feeling of control. Let them play with the garden hose and encourage them to pour water on their legs.

Time

Fears will come and go and your anxious child faces many different challenges in their young life. Thankfully, toddlers generally progress through each anxious stage and tend to move on eventually to the next fear or obstacle. Toddlers will usually move through their bath-time fears *over time*. It is important not to cater fully to their fears, as you do not want to perpetuate a stage that will eventually pass. Conversely, you want to respect the pace at which your child can handle facing their fears. Forcing your child to "get over" their bath fears before they are ready will only make their fears worse.

• • • • • • • • • • • • • • • • •

CHAPTER 7

Fears and Phobias

Mary and David

Mary and David were used to ongoing struggles with their daughter Kelly. It seemed that since she was born they had been going from one challenge to the next. They had already battled eating issues and potty-training struggles, so they were not completely surprised when Kelly started to develop intense fears. Kelly used to walk with her dad every morning before he went to work. It was a nice way for David to spend a little time with Kelly and for them both to get some exercise. Then Kelly started to develop an intense fear of animals, especially dogs. She started to ask her dad to hold her when she saw a dog on the street. If a dog was on their side of the street, Kelly would start to cry and panic. David tried to calm Kelly down during these times, but it seemed as if the only way to calm her was to go back home. David stopped wanting to take Kelly on her walks, as she seemed to get so nervous when he got her ready to go out. She would say repeatedly, "No doggies! No doggies!" and would ask her dad over and over again, "Will we see any dogs?" The situation grew worse when Kelly became fearful of going out at all. Her mom would put her in her car seat and she would start screaming. Her mom realized it must be due to her dog fear when Kelly asked her mom, "Are there dogs where we are going?"

Kelly was also afraid of bugs, bees and birds. If she saw a bee in the backyard, it would take her days to go back outside. At the park, her mom had to sit far away from the pond where the ducks waddled around. She wasn't able to relax or run around with her friends because she always had one eye on where the ducks were congregating. The zoo was completely off limits at this point. The zoo was full of birds feasting on little people's morsels. The birds scared her as they swooped down when her mom got out a snack. Kelly would cry inconsolably when the birds landed near her mom's feet, waiting for a crumb from her messy little toddler hands.

Kelly's fears didn't stop with animals and bugs, as she also had many fears around the house. She was afraid of the dark and wouldn't go into any room by herself. This fear had got worse and she would no longer play in her playroom by herself. Mary noticed that Kelly was right under her feet the entire day. If Mary got up, Kelly would jump up and ask where she was going. If Mary went to the bathroom, Kelly would cry and pound on the door, wanting to come in. Mary couldn't take a shower without Kelly being in her bedroom. Mary began to feel that this wasn't normal! She jokingly told her husband that she felt as if she had a "little stalker."

Kelly would never say what scared her. Her mom would reassure her that she would keep her safe, but it didn't alter Kelly's behavior. Mary and David were baffled by this level of fear and they wondered if something had happened to Kelly while she was at pre-school. They asked the teachers, but they were assured that she had never been hurt or traumatized at school.

Kelly was a fearful child and they continued to be amazed at what would scare her. For the holidays, one of their relatives bought her a toy cat that purred and moved on its own. When Kelly went to touch the toy and it purred, and she cried for over an hour and would not return to the room until they put the toy away.

Mary and David started to get embarrassed by Kelly's behavior. When they took her to church, she would hide behind one of them. When someone talked to her, she would bury her face or just look down. David would prompt her to say hi, but she would refuse. If there were too many people around, Kelly would insist that one of her parents carried her.

Mary hated going to the grocery store with Kelly because inevitably someone would upset her and they would have to leave. One time she thought a woman was staring at her and she kept saying, "Her looking at me!" Eventually Mary had to go to a different section of the store. Another time, a well-intentioned shopper came over to say how pretty Kelly was and tried to talk to her. Kelly started to wail and Mary was embarrassed.

Mary and David made the mistake of taking Kelly to a large amusement park for a family trip. Kelly seemed overwhelmed by the noise, chaos and rides, but it was the people dressed up as characters who triggered the most anxiety. Unfortunately, these "friendly" characters were on every corner and would try to engage Kelly in conversation. It only took a second for these characters to realize she was afraid of them, but by then it was too late. Kelly only needed a small bump in her road to be derailed for the rest of the day. The trip was a disaster and they vowed to never go to any amusement park again. The happiest place on earth—it certainly wasn't!

Holidays had become another source of anxiety. Halloween was by far the worst. Kelly already had an issue with people in costumes and with people wearing masks, but the spooky theme of Halloween didn't help either. It was so bad they didn't dare go trick or treating, but her fears didn't stop there. It was hard to go shopping around Halloween time because the decorations in the stores scared her. Her mom would have to go completely around the Halloween section to avoid a major meltdown.

Kelly

Kelly was a nervous child and as she got older her imagination and fears continued to grow. She worried about everything! Her world became a very scary place, where danger lurked around every corner. She used to enjoy going for walks with her daddy, but once she started noticing the scary dogs on the street it was no longer fun! One time when they were walking down the street, she saw a large dog with a very loud bark. The noise scared her and the dog seemed angry to her. Another time she saw some people talking and the dog jumped up on one of them. What if a dog jumped up on her? She started to scan the street for any scary animals. If she saw one, she'd insist her dad carry her and bring her back home. She felt safe in her daddy's arms.

The world suddenly seemed full of wild bugs, birds and animals that could hurt her. Why had she not noticed all these dangers before? Going outside became a nerve-wracking experience for her. She used to like playing in her backyard, but then she noticed the bugs and flies. Her mom seemed scared of the yellow flies she called "bees" and would swat them away from her if they came too close. This made her even more scared of those yellow flies. She could hear them buzzing around her and she would panic and run inside. Sometimes her mom would say, "It's just a fly." They all looked the same to her.

Going to the park or the zoo wasn't much fun anymore. Loud ducks came up to her with their mouths wide open. She would scream in terror, fearful they were going to eat her. They gathered in groups and she would keep a close eye on them, instead of playing on the playground. It was hard to relax and have fun when there were angry ducks all over the park! The zoo was the same way. Angry, hungry birds would swoop down and try to eat her snack. There were so many trees at the zoo, it was hard to keep track of when a bird might swoop down.

Kelly was also afraid around her house. She was scared of the dark and of shadows. She was worried she might see a bug on the floor. She felt her mom could protect her, so she followed her all around the house. When she couldn't see her mom or her mom went into another room, she'd panic. Without her mom she was not safe! Her mom had told her, "Don't worry, I will keep you safe," and she took that comment literally. She believed as long as she was with her mom, she was safe.

Kelly didn't like crowds of people. People she didn't know scared her. They would pat her head or expect her to talk to them. She didn't know what to say and preferred to cover her face or look away. If a stranger stared at her, she worried they were going to try and talk to her. She didn't like the place they went to on Sundays because it was full of people she didn't know. They were all smiling and patting her. She would get overwhelmed and cry for her mom or dad to hold her. Maybe if she was hiding in her mom's arms, they would leave her alone!

Kelly had a hard time when her parents took her on a trip. They went to a busy place with lots of rides. Huge princesses and other characters she recognized from movies and TV walked around. Some of them didn't have human faces or had legs and arms that were bigger than even her mom's or dad's! They would walk right up to her and try to talk to her. She grew nervous that they might see more of these strange characters so she wanted to be carried most of the time. She didn't know why her parents were getting so mad at her. Didn't they find those strange characters scary too?

When it started to get cold, people would put pumpkins in front of their homes. She didn't like this time of year. Scary monsters and creatures were all over the stores and neighborhood. One night they actually all came to the front door! Her mom and dad told her it was all not real, but it sure looked real to her.

Skill building

As infants move into toddlerhood, they develop a stronger awareness of their environment. As toddlers gain this increased awareness, their level of fear and anxiety can grow. It is normal for the average toddler to be afraid of shadows, monsters and animals. The difference between a typical developmental fear and one of the anxious toddler is the intensity and frequency with which it occurs. The average toddler might be contending with a few fears, but the anxious toddler has a long list of worries.

You may think that a toddler cannot develop coping mechanisms at this stage to overcome their fears, but just the opposite is true. Helping your child understand their worries and how to fight them is a lifelong skill that they need to acquire as soon as possible. The earlier you teach your child these coping mechanisms, the more likely they are to overcome their anxieties in the future. If worries are ignored or you cater to them, they will continue to fester and develop. Your child's worries will compel them to avoid situations, or worse, they will look for you to rescue them. If they successfully avoid things that make them fearful, they are at risk of developing a long list of limitations throughout life. Rescuing your child or conveying a message that they cannot beat challenges without your help may create an unhealthy co-dependency in your relationship that can further debilitate them in the future.

In general, you want to send a message to your child that they have the power to independently face their fears. You want to reframe their thinking and teach them to question their fears. Eventually you want your child to be able to develop methods to self-calm and face their anxieties.

Fear of separation

Toddlers will often try and cope with their anxiety by following you around the house. This is the most common parental complaint I hear in my practice. Does your toddler follow you from room to room? Does your child cry and want to be held all the time? If so, your toddler has already developed coping mechanisms to address their anxiety—just not the type you need or want! Usually toddlers with this type of behavior have developed the irrational belief that they are not safe unless they are near you. More often than not, these children also need to sleep in your bed or need you or someone else to lie with them as they fall asleep. This behavior can be caused by two different issues. The first one is due to their fears. These children do not want to be alone. As long as someone is in the room with them, they feel safe. The other issue has to do with the parent–child relationship and is related to feeling anxious when they are not near their mother. This is called separation anxiety. I will address separation anxiety in detail in Chapter 10. In this chapter we are considering the child who is fearful of being alone in general.

You need to teach your child that they are safe, even if you are not in the same room with them. Initially, you will want to address the underlying anxiety causing them to "shadow" you around the house. You can see specific approaches to various anxieties in the next section of this chapter. Generally, toddlers who shadow their parents are scared of the dark, monsters, shadows, bugs and/or loud noises. More elaborate and sophisticated fears do not usually develop until children are a little bit older.

Be careful about the language you use with your child. Parents will often comfort their child with messages that convey, "I will keep you safe" or "I won't let anything happen to you." As reassuring as these messages sound, the anxious child might misinterpret them as, "You are not safe unless I am with you." A similar, but clearer message might be, "You are safe. Nothing is going to hurt you here."

As with all approaches I have outlined, start off taking small baby steps. Allowing your child to feel secure and empowered is crucial as you build up their ability to face their fears. You do not want them to feel rushed or pressured. Gauge your child's level of fear and alter your pace accordingly. Independence is the ultimate goal, but those skills are not built overnight.

Conversely, do not let your own fears hold your toddler back. Don't underestimate their abilities. Some parents anticipate their child's fears and limit their child's exposure to situations and environments that might cause them distress.

There are times when parents might be pleasantly surprised by their child's ability to cope and overcome challenges. You will never know what your child can overcome if you do not expose them to those challenges. Some discomfort is part of the empowering process. Children are full of pride and excitement when they have successfully faced and confronted a fear. These challenges shape and build their level of self-confidence and self-esteem.

Once you have started to address the specific fear causing the shadowing behavior, you can set up challenges to get your child to feel secure even when you are not in the same room with them. You can play games that encourage separation. Get walkie talkies and go into different rooms to talk. This might take some practicing, as most toddlers have trouble with the concept of walkie talkies. Alternatively you can have them talk to a video baby monitor. You can play Simon Says through the baby monitor, sending them the message that you can still see them through the camera, even though they can't see you.

Moving on to more difficult challenges, you can play a simple game of Hide and Go Seek. Pick obvious spots where parts of your body stick out. The idea is not to scare your toddler, but for them to roam around the house independently searching for you. Another challenge is a scavenger hunt. Hide little toys or candy around the house. When you start this type of challenge, only hide things in the rooms near where you will sit, and as your toddler improves, move your hunt to take in the whole house. Have your child bring back the toys or candy as they find them, providing them with a built in check-in and some unsolicited reassurance. Make sure to comment at the end of each of these challenges that they were able to go into other rooms by themselves and that they were brave and faced their fears. This helps solidify the purpose of the challenges and makes sure the meaning is not lost on your child.

In the next section I have outlined specific fears and phobias anxious toddlers have and approaches to take in those situations.

Shadows and the dark

The most common fear for any child is the fear of the dark. The dark can be scary and ominous. The dark lets imaginations run wild and puts senses on high alert. If your child already has multiple fears, the dark becomes that much scarier. Shadow fears seem to go hand in hand with being afraid of the dark. An active imagination can make a simple, innocuous shadow turn into a scary monster.

Children with an intense fear of the dark will be scared even during daylight hours. They will not go into rooms that are naturally lit. This can stump parents who wonder what is so scary about a naturally lit room in the middle of the day. Anxiety usually doesn't make sense, so the more you try rationally to understand anxiety, the more you'll be confused. Do not try and reason with your child that they shouldn't be scared. This is wasted energy and is inevitably futile. It also makes your child feel as if you do not understand them or their fears.

••••••
125

Teach your child to turn lights on when they enter a room. If they are scared to go into another room say, "Turn the lights on." If your child is too short to turn a light on, have a stool accessible that is light enough for them independently to take around the house. It's a good idea to have a challenge treasure box for your child's fears. Tell them they can earn a treasure if they go into another room for a challenge. Make the challenges easy at first, such as a quick retrieval of something from the other room. Slowly increase the difficulty of the challenges as your toddler shows less fear. Have spontaneous challenges when your child needs or wants something from another room, but wants you to go with them. You can say something like, "I can go with you, but if you take a challenge and do it yourself you can earn a treasure."

To acclimatize your toddler to the dark, have a fun glow party. This can be done in a closet, bathroom or small room.

Get a black light and have everyone wear white t-shirts. You can buy glow sticks and glow jewelry for your glow party. You can get glow-in-the-dark silly string and put glow sticks into balloons to make glow-in-the-dark balloons. The message you are sending your toddler is that the dark can be fun. The more fun you have in the dark, the less fearful they will become. You can buy cheap, battery-operated push lights and place them near your toddler during glow parties. If they get scared they can turn on the light. In general, you can have these lights strategically placed throughout the house, on the wall at your toddler's eye level. You can use removable velcro so the lights can be easily removed when your toddler overcomes some of their major fears.

We talked about shadow play earlier in Chapter 4, but it is worth revisiting in this section. Making shadow puppets and using flashlights that illuminate shapes and pictures on the wall are fun ways to dispel any fears around shadows. If your child is afraid of shadows around the house, ask them where they are so that you can shift objects or show them what is making the shadow. If you notice your child avoiding certain areas of the house, ask them what scares them about the area they are avoiding. If it is because of a shadow, you can help your child learn to explore their environment and alter what is making them fearful. Show them how to play detective and how to discover what is generating the shadow. Help them move objects slightly to alter the shadow and reduce their fear.

Monsters

We addressed the issue of monsters in Chapter 4, but for some children monsters are not just a bedtime issue. There are some children who are afraid of monsters throughout their day. They are afraid to go into another room because they worry that a monster might pop out and eat them.

If your child is afraid to go into rooms alone, ask them what scares them. Walk with them and show them that there are no monsters. Do not over rationalize this issue with your toddler, but do not engage in their make-believe either. In a matter-of-fact way tell your child, as you explore the house, that there are no monsters. Tell them you have never seen monsters and that they are safe. Do not tell your child that you will keep them safe, as this validates the belief that they need to be protected. Do not go into a drawn-out explanation of how monsters are not real, as this will fall on deaf ears at this stage of development.

If your child is into super heroes you can have them create their very own super hero. You can create a story with your child to help motivate them to fight their fears. A story for a child named Zach might go something like this:

> *There once was a boy named Zach. Zach was an ordinary boy with super powers. When Zach got scared, he turned into Super Zach! Super Zach wasn't afraid and he always faced his fears. Super Zach was strong and smart. He knew there was no reason to be afraid. Every time Super Zach faced his fears, he got stronger and stronger. Sometimes a mean guy named Mr. Worry tried to defeat Super Zach. He wanted him to be scared. He told Zach to be scared of the dark. He told him to be afraid of monsters, but Super Zach wasn't going to believe him. Super Zach wanted Mr. Worry to stop bossing him around. He didn't listen to Mr. Worry and he didn't worry about monsters. Mr. Worry couldn't beat Super Zach, so he decided to go bother someone else! Hurray! Super Zach won!*

If your child seems to enjoy the super hero analogy you can use this technique when you are trying to empower them. If your child is afraid to go into another room, you can have a conversation like this:

Child: Can you get my train. It is in the playroom.

Parent: You are brave. You can do it yourself.

Child: Please, please, please. It's dark!

Parent: Do you listen to Mr. Worry or are you Super Zach?

Child: I super hero Zach!

Parent: Then be brave and face your fears.

Child: Uggghhh. Okay.

If you want to have fun with this concept, you can buy your child a generic cape and mask and have them decorate it themselves. When they are feeling scared around the house you can prompt them to put their cape and mask on. This approach makes facing their fears fun and exciting and feeds into their desire for fantasy play. Have them defeat Mr. Worry instead of a monster in order to not further encourage the belief that monsters are a true worry. The concept of Mr. Worry in battling fears is a tool that can be used broadly to address a variety of fears and can be useful for years to come.

Bugs, birds and animals

Things that move and that have mouths are scary to anxious toddlers. They think, "If they have a mouth, they can eat me. If they have legs or wings, they can get to me." That is pretty much the basis of this type of fear.

Bugs

Some children are only afraid of bugs. This fear can be exacerbated by your own reaction to bugs and insects. If your child sees you jumping on chairs when you see a beetle or running away from bugs or bees, you are sending a clear message that these creatures are dangerous. Children can have their own experiences as well. If they have heard loud buzzing in their ears or have felt the pain of a bee sting or an ant bite, they might develop their fears based on this event. For an anxious child, it only takes one experience to make them potentially phobic.

If you are handling a bug inside your home, try to be as calm as possible. I know this can be hard for some people. If you are unable to handle the bug in a calm manner, let someone else in the house take care of it. Do not flush the bug down the toilet! As we talked about in the chapter on bathroom fears, toddlers do not understand that most bugs cannot survive in water. You don't want them to develop a fear that all the bugs you flush down the toilet can crawl back out while they are sitting on it!

When you are outside, show your child how to scoot bugs away with their foot or with a stick. For small, harmless bugs you can make up a narrative as you kneel down to watch it. You can say something like, "Look at this little bug. He is having a busy day. What do you think he has to do today?" Helping personify the bug will start to reduce your toddler's anxiety. Also, seeing you kneel down close to the bug sends a message to your child that you are not afraid of the bug. If your child is afraid of flies and bees you can begin to explain how to tell the difference. You can give your child a fly swatter to shoo away flies. This will make them feel more secure and in control when they are outside.

If your child refuses to go outside due to their fear of bugs, set up challenges where they spend increments of time outside in order to earn a prize from the treasure box. Let your child determine the details of the challenge, so they feel in control. Set up positive, distracting activities outside to keep them entertained during the challenge. You can use bubbles, sidewalk chalk or a sand table to help keep them entertained. Praise them for facing their fears, and reinforce the understanding that going outside is safe and fun.

If your child is not ready for an outside challenge, buy plastic bugs to address the phobia inside. Children with acute bug anxieties will not want to handle plastic bugs either. You can set up the plastic bugs on a table and make up a fun story for your child. Making the bugs fun and personable will help your child feel more comfortable around bugs. Eventually, encourage your child to make up their own story and to touch the bugs themselves. When they have successfully mastered indoor, plastic bug play, try to move to outdoor challenges.

You can also have your child watch TV shows and movies with bug themes. *Miss Spider* is a cute TV series where all the characters are various types of bugs. There have also been some cute bug movies such as *Antz*, *A Bug's Life* and *Bee Movie*.

Birds

Birds can be another scary element in nature. Depending on where you live and how often the birds are fed by humans, they can be very people friendly. Birds, especially at zoos and parks, are used to human encounters and are waiting for their next meal of crumbs. They can come right up to you, pecking near your feet. This may not seem like a big deal to you, but your toddler sees a wild animal with a sharp beak, much closer to their face than to yours.

Instead of telling your child the bird won't hurt them, teach them how to get the bird to leave them alone—this is much more empowering. Show them how to stomp their feet and clap their hands in order to scare the bird away. Toddlers learn more by example than by over-processing issues. Show your child that you are not afraid of the birds and talk to the birds directly, saying something like, "Hi birds! I know you are just looking for food, but my daughter is afraid of you so we are going to have to ask you to leave." Then clap your hands or stomp your feet to show your child how to move the birds away from her.

Cats and dogs

Animals, in particular dogs and cats, can create heightened anxiety for your little one. Dogs often bark loudly and can seem intimidating for small children. Pets can jump up on children and their exuberance can be misinterpreted as aggression. They can scratch and nip at your child inadvertently when being playful. Toddlers don't always know how to handle animals and can illicit a negative reaction from the pet. If your child doesn't have a pet of their own, they are more likely to have an anxious reaction to pets they encounter.

Teach your child how to read animal cues. Tell your child to approach animals slowly in order not to scare them. You can explain to your child that some pets get scared too and that animals need reassurance that *they* are safe. Teach your child to put their hand out when greeting pets. Tell them that pets like to smell and that is one way they get to know people. After a pet smells them, tell your child that the pet might rub up against them wanting to be stroked. You can tell your child that a dog is happy and playful if their tail is wagging and the same is true if a cat is purring.

If your child's fear of pets prevents them from going over to other people's homes, you probably want to actively work on their phobia. If you have a friend or family member with a calm dog or cat, this is a great place to start. Arrange a playdate with your child and the pet. You might have to start by holding your child, depending on their level of fear. Slowly work towards having your child in the same room as the pet. It might help initially to have the pet on a leash, so your child feels there is more control. Do not rush your child, as you want them to feel empowered and not pressured. Eventually, have someone hold the dog or cat as your child puts their hand out for the animal to sniff. Encourage your child to pet the dog or cat. The ultimate goal is to have the pet roam free in the same room as your toddler. This may take a few visits to accomplish, but consistency and frequency are key. Don't feel panicked—some fears take a period of time to get over. Slow and steady will win the race! Just keep visiting the pet on a regular, routine basis so you do not lose any momentum you build.

Once your child has mastered their fears with the calm pet you used above, expose them to new animals. Remind them to put their hand out to greet the pet. They may take a similar amount of time to get used to the new animal. You might have to put some energy towards getting your child comfortable with the animal before they will feel relaxed enough to be near them. If you are at the park or walking down a street and the animal is on a leash, point out that the dog is leashed and cannot run up to them.

If your child is not ready for any of the above challenges, you can start with exposing your child to pretend dogs and cats. There are many realistic and battery-operated pets. Some of these toys interact with the child in a very real fashion, purring or barking when they are stroked. Movies may also be a useful tool in reframing your child's view of pets. TV shows like *Clifford* or *Garfield* or movies that include talking pets may be helpful in changing your child's perspective on animals.

Bouncy houses and playground bridges

Children with spatial issues or who have sensory issues can have fears related to movement and space. This may seem like a random fear, but the world of a toddler is filled with bouncy houses, bouncy slides, trampolines and planked playground bridges. The issue has less to do with heights and more to do with uncontrolled movement. Children with an acute fear of movement are limited on the playground, on playdates and at birthday parties. This can become upsetting for your child, and for you to witness.

When children are uncontrollably bounced up and down in a bouncy house, the inability to control their body can be a scary sensation. Children with this type of fear may initially think they can handle the bouncy house, but will quickly grow upset when someone comes in and makes the floor a moving balloon. Trampolines have a similar effect, but can sometimes be a little less daunting. Trampolines are a bit firmer and do not cave in as much as bouncy houses do. The planked bridge on the playground and the netted rope of a jungle gym have similar effects. Children get a visual cue that they are high up and physical cues that they are not stable. This can be overwhelming for an anxious child with an overactive vestibular system. We will discuss the vestibular system further in Chapter 11 when we go into sensory integration issues.

In order to help your child through these fears you need to be patient. If you try to push them through their fears when they are not ready, they may never get the courage to try the activity again. Help your child feel courageous by being there to hold their hand or catch them. If possible, have your child sit and eventually stand in a bouncy house or trampoline without any other kids in it. It may be a challenge to find an empty bouncy house or trampoline, but sometimes during off hours some indoor playgrounds are pretty desolate. Don't wait for invitations to birthday parties and playdates to desensitize your child, as this is the last place they are going to want to go out of their comfort zone and work on their fears. Giving your child time alone in this environment helps them master the ability to tolerate their own movements and to gain a familiarity with how their jumping and the motions are interrelated. Once your child has completely acclimatized to their own movement (which may take an extended period of time) add your own slow movement to the mix. This gives your child the opportunity to experience what it feels like to have motion outside their control. You can tell them that you will stop whenever they ask you to. Over time, expose

●●●●●●

your child to more opportunities to conquer their fear, while increasing the movement they experience.

For a planked, movable playground bridge, hold your child in your arms as you walk across it. This allows your child to sense the movement of the bridge, without the fear of falling through the cracks. Eventually, scale down to holding their hand, while slowly walking together across the bridge. Some toddlers like to crawl across these bridges first, as it seems less scary and daunting for them. Like the bouncy houses and trampolines, ongoing exposure and time will help your little one conquer this fear. Visits to a park that has a bridge during off hours will help give your child a chance to practice without worrying about being trampled over by other kids.

As with every other fear, ongoing exposure and practice will help your child overcome their fears. Each child will have their own pace and comfort level around facing their fears. It is important to be patient, while giving your child repeated opportunities to confront their fears and eventually overcome them.

Doctors and dentists

Being afraid of going to the doctor or the dentist usually begins after toddlerhood, but very observant, intelligent toddlers can develop fears at this stage. Children with sensory issues who are more sensitive to pain are more likely to make the connection between the doctor's office and shots. Children with oral defensiveness are more likely to have early struggles at the dentist's office.

If your child has a major fear of going to the doctor or the dentist, try to let the doctor or dentist know the situation ahead of time. Although pediatric doctors and dentists are already adept at working with children, they have busy schedules and may not take the time to make your child feel at ease if they don't know there is an issue. Generally, I would advise you to not tell your child about the appointment too far in advance. You don't want them worrying for days about an upcoming appointment. Tell your child an hour or two ahead, giving them some time to process the situation, while not ruining their mood for days. Be honest with your child. If they are scheduled to get a shot and they ask you if they are going to get any shots, tell them the truth. If they ask if the shot will hurt, you can answer with, "It will sting for a second and then it will be all over and you will be fine." Your child will eventually have the shot and realize that it did indeed hurt, so lying to your child can only damage the level of trust they have in you. Have a fun activity scheduled after the appointment. This will help you redirect your child's nervous energy and will help distract them throughout the appointment. You can use the fun activity as a motivator to get them through their appointment by saying things like, "As soon as we are done with this we are going to have so much fun!" This also helps your child link a positive experience (the fun activity) with the negative experience (the doctor visit), taking away some of the stigma for next time.

At home you can help your child with their fears by playing doctor or dentist. They can incorporate their dolls or use you as a patient. You can take turns being the doctor and patient. Try to model the steps and mannerisms of their regular doctor or dentist.

Masks and costumes

As shown in the vignette at the beginning of this story, masks and costumes can be upsetting for some toddlers, especially younger ones. Young toddlers have a hard time differentiating between what is real and what is fake. Costumes and masks can seem very real and they may not realize that the masked "thing" is just an ordinary person underneath.

Most toddlers grow out of this fear, but if it becomes a major issue for your child you can try to address it. Create a dress-up bin and have your child dress up in costumes. Show them what they look like in a mirror and take pictures of them. After they are comfortable, you can start to play dress-up too. Show them what you are going to wear before you put on the costume. Don't forget eventually to use masks, as they are often what makes toddlers the most fearful.

Storms and weather

Similar to the fear of doctors, the fear of weather usually occurs when children are a little bit older. There are, however, very anxious toddlers who develop more advanced fears at an earlier age. At this stage of development, toddler fears are usually limited to the sights and sounds of storms. We discussed how to address storm fears in Chapter 4 when we were covering bedtime issues. The approaches outlined in that chapter would be effective at any time of day and can be used to address general weather fears as well.

Collecting, hoarding and mourning the loss of the couch

Is your toddler a collector? Maybe not the type of collector you want them to be! Anxious toddlers like to collect things. They like rocks, seeds, little pieces of glittery trash, restaurant coloring sheets—you name it, they don't want to throw it away. Some children will even walk around holding a found treasure for days on end. They might insist on sleeping with the item or taking it wherever they go. This can be baffling to some parents, especially when the item they insist on carrying is something like an empty gum wrapper.

Usually this behavior provides toddlers with some sense of security and they typically outgrow treasure collecting. On rare occasions it can lead to more extreme behaviors like hoarding. It is important to not disregard the importance your child places on these treasures. Do not throw away items your toddler has deemed valuable. It is not helpful to tell them that it is trash and that they should throw it away, unless of course it is a safety or hygiene issue! You will not be able to have a rational conversation with your child about this behavior and, if you do, they will feel defensive and anxious that you are going to throw their stuff away. You want to show your toddler respect, while limiting the intensity of this type of habit. I would not recommend fostering this behavior by pointing out or collecting things for your child. As cute as it may seem, it can become an ongoing issue if it is allowed to get out of control.

I recommend you have some sort of treasure box that you designate for your child's treasures. It is nice if it is portable, as some children like to drag their treasures from room to room. The treasure box helps keep their collection contained and, if they are serious collectors, you can limit their loot to what will fit in the box. If they want to add more stuff to their already full box, tell your child that they have to make room by getting rid of some stuff in the box. This helps them learn to let things go, limits their collecting and prevents hoarding behavior.

Some children covet their treasures one day and have completely forgotten about them the next. If your child is like this, you can have a private drawer in your bedroom where you put forgotten treasures. Instead of encouraging collecting, you can curb the behavior by preventing the treasures from being accumulated. Once your child hasn't noticed the missing treasure for a few days, it is probably safe to discard it completely.

You might have to use both of the above approaches. Have a drawer for your toddler to place their treasures in, while putting old or forgotten treasures in your own drawer for future discarding. If your child notices their missing, forgotten item, you will have it available to give them. Most of the time items that are forgotten remain forgotten, but you never know, so keep them until you are confident your toddler won't ask for them.

Children who like to collect may also have a hard time when parents replace or get rid of objects around the house. Anxious toddlers become attached to their surroundings and many of them do not like any changes made in their home environment. Children can get very upset over changes to the furniture, flooring or walls. Some children may become obstinate, refusing to sit on the new couch, insisting you bring the old one back.

Respect your child's attempt to exerting control over the situation, but do not enable their inability to adapt. You can tell your child that they can choose to be uncomfortable and not sit on the new couch, as that is their choice, but the old couch will not be coming back. You can talk to your child about change. The conversation could go something like this:

Child: I want the old couch back!

Parent: I know you miss that couch. It is hard to get used to something new.

Child: Yeah! I don't like new brown couch!

Parent: I know. But our old couch was dirty and not cozy anymore.

Child: No it wasn't! I like it!

Parent: I know you are sad. But the old couch isn't here anymore.

Child: I want it back!

Parent: I know and you might feel that way for a little while and that's okay.

Validate your child's feelings first and let them express how they feel before you move into explaining the situation. In general, this is a good way to communicate with your child. Let them sit with their feelings instead of quickly trying to assuage their pain. It is alright to have unpleasant feelings and as parents we can't always swoop in and take that pain away from our child. Pain and discomfort are part of life's learning process.

As tempting as it may be, I would discourage any enabling behavior such as bringing back the old furniture, giving your child a piece of the carpet you replaced or keeping the old object in the garage where your child can "visit" it. You want to help your child learn to adapt and to develop healthy coping mechanisms. Having them hold on to something old that you want to discard could teach them unhealthy coping mechanisms and could encourage hoarding behavior in the future.

Riding in the car

Some children have a negative reaction about going in the car. This can be for several reasons. Anxious toddlers do not like change or transitions—the car represents both. Also, children with sensory issues do not like to be confined in a car seat. If they are pulling at their seatbelt, they are most likely having a sensory issue.

Always tell your child where they are going and what they can expect. This eliminates the anxiety around the unknown, unless it is a place they have never been. Give your child plenty of warning that you will be leaving, so there is no rush getting them into the car. If they do not like the restriction of the seatbelt, there may not be much you can do about that. You can try and make sure the seatbelt is not unnecessarily tight on their chest and that it is not hitting their bare skin anywhere. If they are particularly sensitive, you can buy a plush seatbelt cover that attaches over the seatbelt.

To make the car ride more exciting and to provide your child with distractions, you can have "car toys" and car entertainment. You want your child to associate the car with fun, thereby reducing their resistance to the car in general. You can get window gel clings to entertain your child. These are gel-like stickers that stick to windows and they can be found at most major stores, especially around any holiday. Your child can decorate their window as you drive. The stickers can be peeled off easily and saved for future use. You can also have one or two toys that are designated just for the car. Your child will be excited to be in the car, as this is the only time they get to play with those toys.

Water, pools and baths

Fear of water is a common phobia in toddlerhood. Most toddlers will eventually overcome this fear. We discussed the fear of baths in Chapter 6 and you can review that chapter for ideas around water fears in general. It is best to expose your child to water frequently if they are showing some apprehension or fear about it. You don't want to force your child to get into water, but you *do* want to give them as many opportunities as you can to be exposed to water. The longer you allow your toddler to avoid water, the stronger their fears will grow.

Slowly try to get your toddler acclimatized to water by creating the least intimidating environment for them. This might be a plastic tub of water in the backyard or a small inflatable pool for them to put their feet in. You can fill up the tub or pool with a few inches of water in the summer time, giving them a chance to experiment with the water. Add fun toys and bath body paint to enhance the enjoyment of water play and to keep your toddler playing in the water longer. Always stay with them when they are near water—even a few inches of water. As your toddler's level of confidence grows, continue adding more water each time they play.

"Mommy/Daddy and Me" swim classes can be helpful as well. Many swim schools offer classes where you can go into the pool with your toddler. Usually these are fun, structured classes where your child sings songs and gets used to basic water sensations. Do not sign up for any swim classes that have a "sink or swim" approach to teaching. Tough love is not the way to teach your anxious toddler how to swim. If a swim instructor forces your child to dunk their head in the water, they may never want to try swimming again. Slow and steady wins the race with this issue. Find swim classes that are nurturing and supportive.

Automated toys

Toys that move on their own can be scary for the young, anxious toddler. Anything that is unpredictable in their environment can be viewed as a potential threat. Show your toddler where the on/off button is for the toy. Help them learn how to switch off their toys when they are scared.

Some children just aren't ready for an animated toy, especially if it looks too realistic. If your child is unsettled by a moving toy, put it away and save it for later. You'd be surprised how quickly your toddler will go from one stage to another. What was once a scary toy might be their favorite toy only a few months later!

Loud noises

Loud noises are one of the top fears for any toddler. Loud noises are scary because they are unpredictable and sometimes mysterious. Toddlers are just learning about their environment and haven't matched up every sound to its origin. Help your child play detective and have them discover what the sounds are that tend to scare them. If they are scared of the garbage truck, run to the window with your child when the truck is on your street. Show your child what the sound is and what the truck is doing on the street. The next time they hear the garbage truck encourage them to run to the window and watch it. The fear of this sound will lessen over time, as they grow familiar with the sound and the purpose of the truck.

A key component to anxiety around sound has to do with auditory hypersensitivities. We will go into further detail regarding sensory processing issues in Chapter 11. Children who are more hypersensitive to sound hear noises amplified. A vacuum cleaner can sound like a thunderous noise to your child. This can make cleaning the house, using the garbage disposal or even turning on the washing machine a challenge! Show your child what is making the noise. It might help to have them wear kid headphones that cancel out the intensity of the noise. Let them turn the vacuum cleaner, garbage disposal or washing machine on and off. This gives them a feeling of control and power. When you are going to do a household activity that usually upsets your toddler, let them know in advance. You can offer them the choice to wear headphones or to go into another room. Do not alter your usual behavior, as you want your child to adapt to the noises. Usually children will develop a higher tolerance for such household sounds as they get older.

For noisy events such as fireworks, monster truck shows and music festivals, you can bring wax ear plugs to help lessen the intensity of noise your child is hearing. Wax ear plugs are better than foam ear plugs, as they can be molded more easily to little ears. Headphones are probably equally effective, but if your child has sensory issues they might struggle with having something on their head for an extended period of time. Also, you are trying to develop coping mechanisms that can be used as they get older and in a multitude of environments. As your child reaches school age, they will probably feel that headphones are too conspicuous and they might prefer the more subtle approach of wax ear plugs to drown out annoying and distracting noises.

Strangers

Usually as toddlers get older they become more friendly and trusting of those around them. There are some toddlers, however, who remain very fearful of anyone outside their immediate family. For these families, simple playdates, parties or visits to the park can be a harrowing experience.

If your toddler is showing distress around strangers this might be an issue you want to start addressing before they enter pre-school or kindergarten. Most toddlers will outgrow their fear of those they do not know. There are, however, a small number of children, especially those who refuse to talk at all to anyone outside their family, who may have an acute issue called selective mutism. We will cover selective mutism in Chapter 12, when we discuss what to look for in the future.

Help your child by taking small steps to make them comfortable around people they do not know. If you have been pumping up the rhetoric on stranger danger, this may be the time to put that conversation on pause. If your child hides around your legs or in your arms, do not force them to talk to the other person, but do not enable the behavior further by speaking for them. Prompt your child to take baby steps. If they are hiding, you can tell them, "You don't have to talk, but please stop hiding." This creates a safe space for your child, where they know there are no expectations placed on them. Once your child is comfortable with not hiding, you can step up your expectations by saying, "You don't have to say anything, but at least smile or wave if someone talks directly to you."

Encourage your child to continue taking more steps towards being friendly. Your child may never be fully comfortable or verbose with those they don't know, but you want them to be able to be courteous and anxiety-free around others. We will discuss social interaction with peers in Chapter 8.

Crowds

Crowds can be overstimulating and chaotic for a sensitive child. The loud noises, the hustle and bustle of people walking everywhere and the different smells of food can cause sensory overload for some toddlers. Amusement parks, water parks, fairs, festivals and concerts are just a few places where your toddler can experience sensory overload.

For some parents, it isn't worth going to a place where their child becomes a miserable mess. I agree. Crowds aren't for everyone and it isn't necessarily a situation your child may ever feel comfortable in. They may never like crowds. However, there may be a time you need or want to go into a crowded situation with your sensitive little one. Other children in the family may want to do a fun activity and it isn't fair that everyone else misses out because of one child. To stack the deck in your favor, bring a stroller. Toddlers tend to feel more comforted within the protection of a stroller. It also gives them the impression of space around them, so they do not feel trampled on or pushed by others. Also, they know they can't lose you because they are confined to the stroller that you are pushing. If your child gets visually overwhelmed, you can bring a book so they can look down and limit their visual stimuli in order to "reset." If your child is sensitive to noise, you can bring wax ear plugs to limit the intensity of noise around them. If your child responds well to calming music, you can bring music and headphones to help soothe them. Try and keep to one side of the crowd so your child doesn't feel surrounded on both sides. Give your child periods of less stimulation by going away from the crowds and allowing the child time to regroup.

Failure and perfectionism

You probably think perfectionism doesn't start until a child is school aged, but if you pay close enough attention, you can see these behaviors start in toddlerhood. Some children expect that they should know everything straight out of the womb! They get easily frustrated when they can't learn something quickly or master a task in a few short steps. This is a key time to help your child learn the concept of *practice makes perfect.* If you swoop in and complete the task for them, you are inadvertently communicating to them, "You're right, you can't do it. You need my help." When this is done on a repeated basis, your child is more likely to have a "give up" attitude and will learn to look around for others to complete their work for them.

As strange as this may sound, these lessens are being learned in simple tasks, such as getting dressed or putting on their shoes. How many times have you watched your toddler struggle to put their leg through the wrong pant hole or to put a cap back on a marker? Encourage your child with words like, "You can do it!" and "It's okay, you were almost there. Try again." If your child refuses to try again, get them started, but do not complete the task for them. For example, put their foot through the right pant hole and say, "Okay, try again. I know you can do it!" or put the cap on the marker, but do not snap it and say, "Okay, now push down. Yay! You did it. See, you can do it all by yourself!" If your child gets frustrated when doing a difficult task, explain to them, "Everyone has to practice when they are learning in order to get better. I didn't know how to do that either, but I practiced and practiced and never gave up! You can do that too!"

If your child wants everything perfect, make an effort to make things less than perfect once in a while. If they tell you how to draw something or they tell you that you are doing something "incorrectly," use that opportunity to tell them that everyone does things differently and that there is no right or wrong way of doing things. Reiterate to them that things do not have to be perfect and that making mistakes is part of learning. When you are doing crafts with your child, don't work too hard on getting your craft as perfect as possible. Having mom or dad's craft always looking impeccable can be discouraging for your child. Focus on supporting them as they do their art work. Make comments as you observe your child doing art, such as, "I like the way you added that color" or "That is a beautiful picture!" If your child gets frustrated about how their project turned out, you can make comments like, "Well I like it and I am going to hang it up!"

Dust and dust bunnies

If you have tile or wood floors in your home, you are probably familiar with dust bunnies—those annoying dust and hair balls that gather in the corners and under furniture. To parents, these dust balls are just a cleaning inconvenience, but to the anxious toddler they can be viewed as scary, furry creatures that can cause complete panic!

If your child is having a strong reaction to dust bunnies, don't accommodate them by making sure they never come into contact with one. Like all the other fears we've discussed, you want to help your child confront this in order to move past it. Pick one up and explain to your child what makes up a dust bunny. Pull one apart so they can see that it is just full of dust and hair. Encourage them to hold one and pull it apart. Invite them to be a helper when you are cleaning and have them throw them in the garbage. If they are very fearful, offer the task as a challenge where they can earn a prize. Although your child can obviously survive in life without getting rid of their fear of dust bunnies, you want to encourage them to address fears as they meet them and not accumulate an ever-growing list of new fears and phobias as they get older.

Falling down stairs

Some cautious, anxious toddlers have a fear of falling down the stairs. This may be due to a tumble they once had or just the fear of tumbling. Children don't need a traumatic event to have a fear. This fear is hard to detect and some parents are not aware their child even has this issue. If your child demands that you pick them up when they go up the stairs or scoots on their bottom when they go up and down, that might be an indication that they have a fear around the stairs.

It is important to not accommodate their fear. I would discourage giving in and picking them up. If they need to scoot up and down the stairs that is still one step closer to walking than if you were carrying them. Always try to encourage as much independence as you can. You can help them address their fears by saying something like, "It seems as if you are afraid you might fall. If it is scary, you can scoot on your bottom for now, but I am not going to pick you up." Teach your child to hold the wall or, if they are able to, the railing. When they have no fear while scooting, encourage them to stand up and walk up and down the stairs.

Fear after minor trauma

Anxious toddlers are like little elephants—they have amazing and unforgiving memories. They remember how to get to grandma's house, they remember what you promised them and they definitely remember all of their traumatic experiences. When a minor trauma occurs to an anxious toddler, they are much more likely to try and avoid that situation in the future.

After a minor trauma, such as tripping or falling off a swing, try to expose your child to that situation again. The longer your child avoids it, the more ingrained the fear will become. For example, if your child went down a slide too fast and slid right off the end, your goal would be to encourage them to go down the slide again. To make them feel more secure you can tell them that you will be at the bottom to catch them if they are going too fast. It might take some coaxing, but if your child is able to "redo" the event without the trauma, it is less likely that there will be any residual traumatic effects in the future.

If a child falls or hurts themselves, take care of their cuts and scrapes, and then go back and do the same activity again. You can make this a fun game by saying, "Let's press the rewind button and go back and redo that! This time you won't get hurt!" You want your child's last memory of the situation to be a positive one. This will help negate any bad emotions they might carry with them moving forward.

General approaches to fears

Explore the origin of the fear

This may seem obvious, but in order to help your child overcome their fears, first you have to know what scares them. I have worked with many parents who can describe in detail what their child's avoidant behavior looks like (for example, he screams when we get into the car, he won't sleep on his own), but cannot tell me why their child is avoiding that situation. You cannot come up with approaches on how to get your child not to scream in the car until you know what is causing his screaming. Does he not like his seatbelt? Is he afraid that you will take him to the doctor? Who knows? Do not assume you know what is causing your child's fears, as they will often surprise you with their answers.

In order to investigate what makes your child afraid, pay attention to what kind of questions they ask. When a child asks repeated questions that evoke reassurance, they are usually anxiety related. For instance, if your child is asking, "We go in car? I no want to go in car!" that can be confusing, but the question indicates there is fear around going in the car. Instead of dismissing their question, ask open-ended feeling questions such as, "Why don't you want to go in the car?" or "What's the worst thing about the car?" By taking the time to proactively investigate your child's fears about the car, you will avoid a complete meltdown when the time comes to get your child into the car. At that point, your child's emotions will be heightened to such a degree they will not be able to process what they are afraid of and you will most likely have a stand off and an ensuing meltdown.

Observe play

Observe your child's play themes. Your child may have themes in their play that will give you an indication of what is consuming their little mind. Do not take your child's play literally, as most play is an exaggeration of themes and emotions they have in real life and some play can be disturbing. If your child has a specific avoidant behavior, for example about going to the toilet, incorporate that into their play. Give them a few dolls and a toy toilet and see what type of play they do. If you are trying to assess what makes your child afraid, do not join in the play and alter the flow and theme of their story line.

Watch what they watch

Observe what your child watches on television. TV shows and movies can generate sudden fears that can catch parents off guard. If your child has a sudden and unexplained fear after watching TV, ask them directly, "Did you see something on TV that was scary?" Sometimes even the most innocuous TV shows and movies have themes that may unexpectedly upset your child. Movies like *Finding Nemo* and *Frozen* may seem harmless enough, but an anxious child might fixate on the loss of a parent and may become scared that they will lose their parents too. An anxious child cannot live in a bubble and you cannot always predict what will upset your child. You shouldn't have to preview episodes of *Sesame Street* before you allow your child to view them, but be cautious of any show that borders on scary. If your child watches a show and often covers their eyes or appears nervous, this is a clear indicator that the show is too scary for them.

If you have a very anxious child who is easily affected by media, avoid having any TV on that is not child-centered. Even if your child is playing, they may catch a glimpse of a grown-up show, the news or a commercial that has scary or confusing images. I have worked with many young children who have intense fears and phobias solely based on watching the news or seeing trailers for horror movies. Those trailers can be pretty scary!

Remain balanced in your approach

Once you know *why* your child is scared, it is time to roll up your sleeves and try to help them overcome those fears. Parents are at risk of falling into two extreme categories when it comes to dealing with their toddler's fears—overly enabling and accommodating, or punitive and apathetic towards their child's struggles. The best approach is not to accommodate your child's avoidant behavior, but to be aware of when your child has had enough. This is a balancing act that can be tricky for any parent. Don't beat yourself up if you periodically accommodate your child's fears. Life is busy, little ones get tired and parents get tired. There will be times when you are just making it through the day and you do not have the energy to focus on helping your child face their fears. Also, there will be days where you are over-zealous about being supermom or dad and want your child to face their fears. They, unfortunately may not feel as zealous about your endeavor and you may push them too far before you realize it. None of us is a perfect parent. I have never met a perfect parent, including myself. So, we all mess up. You might have to dial it back at times or push yourself harder to not overly accommodate—constant adjustment is part of the process!

Empower through play

Once you know what scares your child, you can teach them to address their fears through their play. If your child has anxiety themes in their play, you can jump into their play and introduce an empowering tone. This may sound confusing, but it is actually really simple. Let's say your child is afraid of the toilet. You have them play with a few dolls and a toy toilet. You can take a doll and encourage your child to be the parent. Speak for the doll, saying things like, "I don't want to go to the toilet! I'm scared!" Your child will be in a position of control and usually will start to encourage the doll, "You can do it!" Sometimes they will mimic what you normally tell them. This power shift helps your child be the voice of reason and inspiration for their *own* fears. This approach will not fully resolve the fear, but it is a helpful tool to have in your toolbox and will help your child process their fears from a different perspective.

Empowerment through storytelling

Another type of approach is through storytelling. Toddlers love a story, especially with them in it! They will learn a life lesson more quickly if it is told in story form. When your child is having a hard time, sometimes it is better to break out into a story than to over-process the issue with them. Let's say your child is nervous about going to swim class. Instead of talking about it, you could say something like this:

Let me tell you a story. There once was a boy named John (insert your child's name here). He wanted to learn how to swim, but the water made him very scared. He had a nice teacher and there were some very nice kids in his class. Although he was scared, he knew that he wanted to learn how to swim. He loved going to the pool in the summer and it would be so much fun to be able to go down the water slide. John said to himself, "I am not going to let my fears boss me around!" John reminded himself he had a nice teacher who would never let anything bad happen to him. He also remembered that his mom would be right by the pool watching. John was ready to face his fears! He was ready to be a swimmer!

Telling your child an empowering story may not make them act like the character you are speaking about, but it is motivating. It also validates your child's feelings and offers them new ways to think about their problem.

Deep breathing

In general, teaching your child how to deep breathe can be helpful. When children are anxious they tend to take more shallow breaths and, if they are really panicky, they can start to hyperventilate. Bubbles are a wonderful tool to help little kids learn how to deep breathe. Children get a visual picture of the breath as their bubble grows. In order to blow bubbles, you have to control your breath. Children will start to regulate their breathing in order to blow a successful bubble.

Be aware of little ears

I am sure at times you will talk to your partner, your best friend or your relatives about the struggles you are having with your anxious toddler. It is good to get support and guidance from those around you. When discussing your child's fears with others though, be sure to check that little ears can't hear you. All too often parents do not realize how much their children listen to what they say. A child can play and listen at the same time. Just because your child looks engaged in an activity, it doesn't mean they are not listening to your conversation. For the sensitive child this could be pretty damaging to their progress and their self-esteem. You don't want them to hear the struggles you are having with their anxiety, or the stress it is causing you. Even if you are an open family and like to discuss things all together, try not to have an adult conversation about your child with them in earshot.

In general, I would be cautious about what you talk about around your child. Frequently parents will talk on the phone, to their spouse or to friends about what is happening in the news or the weather. They might discuss financial struggles, marital difficulties and other hardships. Young children don't have the capacity to fully comprehend the content of an adult conversation and they might glean something that is not true from what they overhear. For instance, if they hear you and your spouse fighting, they might fear it is their fault. Children at this age are very egocentric.

CHAPTER 8

• • • • • • • • • • •

Playtime and Social Anxiety

Vicky and Don

Vicky and Don have always described their second son Jake as a cautious child. He was slow to talk and didn't start walking until he was confident he could walk without falling. When Jake turned one, he started to show apprehension around people outside his immediate family. When people approached Jake at the grocery store, he would lower his head and hide his eyes. At first Vicky just thought Jake was going through a stage. Their other son had been shy for a period of time when he was little and he eventually became very friendly with everybody. But Jake's apprehension around other people continued to grow and Vicky was forced to accept that rather than being a stage, this might be Jake's personality. It was hard for Vicky to relate to Jake because she was so friendly and outgoing. She hated to admit it, but his behavior embarrassed her because she often felt he was being rude and unfriendly for no reason.

Vicky started to fear playdates, as they seemed more work than they were worth! When Vicky got to the playdate, Jake would be stuck to her leg. He would insist that his mom picked him up if anyone tried to talk to him. Vicky got used to speaking for Jake. She would often tell people, "Sorry, he's really shy!" She would try to cajole Jake into talking with her friends, saying, "Jake, tell Sarah hello. She wants to see your pretty eyes. Show her your pretty eyes." Her friends would pipe in, "Oh Jake, you have pretty eyes. I never get to see your eyes because you are always hiding them. Can you show me your eyes?" Jake would usually bury his face even further into his mom's shoulder. Eventually, Vicky would give up and just hold Jake the whole time and speak for him. Her friends would approach him and ask him, "Do you want a cookie?" and Vicky would answer, "A cookie would be nice." She was embarrassed by her child and although she didn't want to, she couldn't help comparing Jake to all the outgoing little toddlers around her. She would often think, "Who is this foreign little creature holding onto my leg for dear life?"

Don understood Jake much better than Vicky. After all, Don was a reserved, quiet man. Vicky always joked that Don could go for days without talking. Don would laugh and say if he didn't have anything important to say, he'd rather not say anything at all. Vicky and Don were a good match, as Vicky liked to talk and Don liked to listen. They always felt as if they complemented each other in that way. Don would tell Vicky, "Jake's just like me, there is nothing wrong with that," but Vicky would insist that they needed to do something to fix this "problem." Don would tell Vicky to just leave Jake alone and let him warm up in his own time, but that did not sit well with Vicky. It was the one topic that they argued over.

When Don took Jake to the grocery store, he handled well-intentioned strangers with a friendly but firm interaction. One time an overly friendly lady reached for his son's hand in the check-out line and he saw his little boy put his hands over his face. Don thought, some people just don't understand kids. The lady said, "Peek-a-boo, I see you!" Don politely said, "He is a little slow to warm. It is probably best that you let him be." The lady pulled her hand back abruptly and said, "Oh," looking hurt and confused. Don didn't let these type of interactions bother him. He understood his child and it was more important that he stood up for Jake than worried about what some stranger at the grocery store thought of them. He wished Vicky could see it that way.

Holidays were a nightmare for Vicky. She had a large, outgoing and noisy family and they always had big holiday get togethers at her parents' house. She had always enjoyed these celebrations, as it was her time to reconnect with her siblings and spend time with their kids. Once Jake was old enough to walk, the holidays started to feel awkward for Vicky. She'd tell Jake in the car, "Please be nice to your grandma and grandpa. When we go in, give them a kiss and a hug. Do you understand? Don't be rude! They bought you lots of presents this year and if you want any of them, you'd better be nice! Understood?" Vicky knew she was being perhaps a little harsh, but it was just so awful to watch Jake snub her parents in such a hurtful way. Don would tell Vicky privately that he didn't feel as if it was a good idea to force Jake to hug and kiss her relatives. "Why can't you just let him be?" he'd say.

Inevitably, Jake would walk in and he would be surounded by loving, exuberant relatives, demanding hugs and kisses. "Come here Jakie!" they would say. "Give me a kiss!" they would demand. Jake would cling to his mom's shoulders, hugging her tightly. Vicky would get frustrated and would put him down and scold him. Usually at this point, Don would silently take Jake to a quiet room in the house, where he would just rock him and hum. Eventually Jake would stop crying and Don would say, "I hear they've got a new bunny. You want to go outside and check it out?" To which Jake would enthusiastically nod a yes.

Vicky was determined to help Jake through his social struggles; after all, he was already three and should have outgrown this behavior a long time ago! She decided that playdates might be more successful if she had them at her house. She had read that children are normally more comfortable on their own "turf" and perhaps that would help Jake be friendlier. When Vicky's friends arrived, Jake ran into his bedroom. Vicky told him that if he didn't stay in the playroom with his friends, he'd have to go to bed early that night. She closed off his bedroom and forced him back into the playroom. Jake sat in the corner playing with his red car, one of his favorite toys. Another child, saw the red car and grabbed it from Jake's hands. "Car! Vroom! Vroom!" the other child exclaimed. Jake's face turned beet red and then he gave a very high-pitched scream. Everyone came rushing into the room. "What's the matter?" Vicky asked frantically. She checked to see if Jake was hurt. "Why are you crying, Jake?" she asked. He just pointed. Vicky looked at where he was pointing and saw the other child moving the red car back and forth on the carpet. Vicky was mortified. "Jake, you have to learn to share," she informed him. He got very upset and grabbed all of the other cars he could fit into his hands and ran off, trying to get back into his room. Needless to say, Vicky decided not to have playdates at her house ever again. She didn't think it was possible, but playdates at her house were even worse than those at someone else's home!

Jake

Jake liked to observe. He was not one to jump quickly into any situation. He took his time learning new things and it took him a long time to feel comfortable in new situations. People he didn't know well made him nervous. They would get really close to his face or touch his hair. He hated it when they touched his hair. When his mom took him to the store, he'd start to feel scared. People always wanted to talk to him in this place. He tried to look away from people, but it seemed as if no matter what he did, they still tried to talk to him. They would touch his hair and say he had cute curls. He'd wiggle uncomfortably in the shopping cart and cover his eyes. He always thought that if he closed his eyes they would disappear. "He's just shy," he always heard his mom say. What does shy mean. Am I shy? Nobody was going up to my mom touching her hair. I am sure she wouldn't like it either. He hated it when his mom told him to say hi. He didn't want to look at them. He didn't want to speak. If he spoke they might ask him more questions and then they wouldn't go away. The more his mom coaxed him, the more he'd try to disappear into her shoulder.

He hated playdates. To him playdates meant people in his face and his mom getting angrier with him. She was always very quiet on the way home from playdates. He felt as if she was mad at him. He didn't like talking to his mom's friends. They made him more uncomfortable than the strangers at the store. At least the strangers at the store eventually walked away. He felt as if his mom's friends never left him alone. "Let me see your eyes," they would say over and over again. Leave my eyes alone, he'd think! Why do they want to see my eyes anyway? Was something wrong with his eyes? His mom would always tell him that he was being rude. He was confused. What was he doing to be rude? He hadn't even said anything. He wished she never took him to these playdates. Couldn't he play at home? After all, his favorite toys were all at home!

Jake did not like going to his grandma's house, especially when there were lots of people there. His grandma's house was worse than the store or playdates! Everyone wanted to kiss his face and squeeze him so hard. His mom would yell at him to kiss and hug everyone. He didn't like to smell their breath and some of them smelled weird. They were loud and would forcefully pick him up. He would do anything not to go to his grandma's home. Usually he'd start crying and his mom would get so mad at him. He wasn't trying to upset her. He just felt that he couldn't breathe. Luckily his dad usually rescued him when he got like this. He would take him to a quiet place and that helped him start to relax. At least his grandma had recently got a bunny! That made it a little more exciting to go over to her house.

One day Jake's mom announced that they were going to have friends come over. Over here? Jake was confused as to why her friends were coming to their house. They had never had people come over to play before. When people started coming to the house, Jake started to feel scared. Kids were trying to talk to *him and he didn't know what to say. He would ignore them and hug his mom's leg. She would gently push him off her leg and tell him to go and play. He eventually tried to escape by going to his room. It was nice and quiet until his mom found him and got angry. She closed his bedroom door and told him he wasn't allowed to go back in there. Where would he sleep? All of his toys and clothes were in there? Why couldn't he go in there? He went back into the playroom and started playing with his favorite red car. At least his favorite cars were out here in the playroom. Maybe if he turned around no one would see him and they'd leave him alone. He thought he had successfully disappeared, until a little boy came up from behind him and grabbed his car right out of his hands! He thought, I can't let him have my favorite car! Jake started to panic and before he knew it, a high-pitched scream was emanating from his mouth. His mother came over at first with a look of concern on her face. Oh good, Jake thought, my mom is just as upset about my car as I am. He tried to calm down to talk, but he couldn't get the words out. He pointed in the direction of his shiny red car. His mother's face melted with disappointment and her look of concern was quickly replaced with a look of anger. What had he done to make his mom angry? His car was taken. That wasn't his fault! His mom yelled at him to stop crying and told him to share. Is that what sharing meant? He was confused. If that was what she meant when she kept saying "share" he didn't want any part of it! Jake was sad and quiet the rest of the time and was so relieved when everyone finally left. His mother exclaimed that they would never do that again, and he wholeheartedly agreed with her!*

Social anxiety versus separation anxiety

It is important to differentiate social anxiety from separation anxiety. The end result for both types of anxiety is a clingy child, but the cause of the problem is quite different depending on which type of anxiety we are actually talking about. Approaches on how to handle social anxiety and separation anxiety are vastly different, therefore it is very helpful to know which one it might be. Social anxiety is, in simple terms, the fear of being around other people. Separation anxiety is the fear of being separated from the parent, regardless of the environment. An easy way to distinguish between these two types of anxieties is to observe your child's behavior at home. If they follow you from room to room and they need to be right next to you, this is most likely separation anxiety. Another indicator that it might be separation anxiety rather than social anxiety is if your child is fine around others as long as you are in the same room. Children with social anxiety will still exhibit signs of distress, even when you are present in the room. Separation anxiety and social anxiety are not mutually exclusive, so a child can struggle with both issues. Separation anxiety will be discussed in more detail in Chapter 10, but for this chapter we will continue to focus on social anxiety.

Social cautiousness

A socially cautious child shows sign of distress and anxiety around adults and children they are not comfortable with. If your child is socially cautious, you are probably well aware of this fact already. They probably hide their face in your legs and refuse to talk to those around you in social situations. Social anxieties can be mild or acute. Your child might be slightly uncomfortable and reserved around other children and adults or in a complete state of panic. Some children have a heightened anxiety around only adults or only children. This is noticeable by observing how they engage with one group and shut down with the other. Many socially cautious toddlers are anxious around all ages.

As you observed in the vignette at the beginning of this chapter, parents have different approaches and tolerance levels for their child's social cautiousness. I highlighted two differing parenting styles in the vignette. Both parents had good intentions for their child, but different opinions on how to help him. Vicky had a forceful approach to fixing her son's issues, while Don had a more passive approach. I often encounter couples with opposing opinions on their child's anxiety who therefore have completely opposite parenting styles. This can be confusing and counterproductive for the child. Finding a balance and a middle ground where you and your spouse are both comfortable is key to parenting successfully.

An extroverted mother may have a hard time with her introverted child. I have had many extroverted parents voice bafflement over how their child could be so quiet. Some parents even question whether they did something wrong to cause such introversion. Like many other aspects of the personality, people are born with a certain predisposition to behave in a certain way. Our environment can reinforce these attributes or can shape the personality in a different direction. You cannot forcefully try to alter your child's personality, as this might have the counterintuitive effect of actually reinforcing the very behavior you are trying to change. However, gently coaching your child in social situations will help improve their social skills and can alter the level of social anxiety they might feel in the future.

Talkative, friendly parents are at risk of being the voice of their quiet children. Parents may not have the patience or may be too embarrassed to let questions directed towards their child go unanswered. They may get used to talking for their children. This can be easier for both parents and children. The only risk in talking for your child is that they can grow very dependent on this social crutch. They can begin to think, "I don't need to talk because my mom will talk for me." It might be hard not to always talk for your child, especially for those who are completely silent around others, but try to limit the frequency of how often you are your child's voice. Sometimes children will speak if we give them time and do not fill in the silence with our own voices.

Conversely, if you are a quieter parent, you may be inadvertently modeling social avoidance. If you do not make eye contact with those around you or you have a hard time talking with strangers, your child might be observing your behavior. You might be more reluctant to encourage your child to be social when you yourself have a hard time being friendly. You can help your child the most by getting slightly out of your comfort zone and being friendly yourself. This might be as simple as saying hi or smiling to others as you walk past them.

Vicky and Don's son would have benefited from a combination of both Vicky and Don's styles of parenting. Their son Jake would have opened up more socially if he was not put on the spot and forcefully told to engage with those around him. Contrarily, if Jake was completely left to his own devices he would never develop the skills he needed to make him more comfortable in social situations. Jake needed to feel supported and understood. Once Jake felt that his feelings were understood by his parents, they could have coached him and walked him through various social situations. They could have also better prepared and protected him around well-intentioned but overwhelming friends and family. How to handle friendly strangers

Strangers love toddlers and they actively show it! Unlike you or me, who can walk unnoticed through the mall or grocery store, your child is a magnet for unsolicited oohs, aahs and hellos. Welcome to the world of a cute toddler. Most children are unfazed by the doting behavior of others, but for the socially anxious child, it can cause intense panic.

In order to help your child, you have to be a protective barrier from those exuberant strangers. Some strangers may be too loud or too touchy-feely for your child. Your ultimate goal is to provide your child with positive and successful social interactions. The more frequently your child has positive interactions, the more comfortable they will feel in the next situation. If you have a pushy adult invading your child's space, the child is more likely to feel anxious the next time they see an approaching adult.

Everyone has different degrees of comfort when it comes to setting boundaries and limits for those around them. Many socially anxious toddlers have socially anxious parents. Being anxious yourself can be an additional barrier to setting limits for those who approach your child. Sometimes having an idea of what you would say in those type of situations may help you have the courage to say it when the time comes. Below are some phrases that might help set limits with an overly friendly stranger:

> He's slow to warm up, (to your child) aren't you? Would you mind not talking to him?

> Sorry, he doesn't like to talk to strangers.

> He likes to watch people before he's ready to talk, (to your child) don't you?

If someone continues to try and engage with your child after you have set the above boundaries, politely say you are in a bit of a hurry and continue on your way. As you can see in two of the three examples, you can talk to the child as you are explaining their behavior. Including your child in the conversation helps show them that you are aware they are a part of the conversation, even though they are quiet.

Be careful what you say to others, as your little one is listening too. Your child is slowly starting to define their personality by how you are describing them. If you tell everyone that your child is shy, they will define themselves as shy as well. Once a child labels themselves as being a certain way, there is less desire to change or alter that behavior. I have had many children come into my office and tell me, "I am just shy." Normally my response is something like, "You don't seem shy to me. You are friendly and talkative in here." At that point the child may recognize the discrepancy in the label versus their behavior and say something like, "I am shy when I don't know what to say." This realization helps broaden the child's view of how they act and gives them permission to act differently in different situations.

I am not a big proponent of forcing toddlers to talk to strangers; however, it is important to instill basic manners. You might say to your child, "You don't have to talk to people you don't know, even if they want you to talk. It is polite, however, to not look down when someone is talking to you. You can just smile or stare at them, but at least try to look at them." I would not have this discussion in front of strangers. It can be a discussion you might choose to have when you are going to the store or when you know you will be out in public. You can even set up a fun challenge where they can earn something from a treasure box if they make eye contact with strangers. Once your child is on the spot in an active situation with a friendly stranger, I would not use that time to encourage them to alter their behavior. The pressure of having the stranger in their space is enough for the socially anxious child and they do not need you to add to their stress in that moment by encouraging eye contact.

Interacting with relatives and family friends

Your approach to dealing with friendly relatives and family friends will look completely different from the approach we discussed for strangers. These are people you want your child to be friendly around in order to grow their relationship, so it is important to walk your child through these social interactions.

The initial step consists of guiding your family and friends on how to best approach your little one. You want to maximize your child's positive social experiences, even if they are somewhat orchestrated at this point. Your child is in the initial stages of developing lifelong social skills. You want these formative years to be as positive and successful as possible. Your child may not be wired to be the most outgoing, gregarious person in the room, but you don't want their social apprehension to become a barrier that will hold them back in life.

Talk to your family and friends about how to approach your child. You can tell them something like:

> *(Insert your child's name) takes time to warm up. Please don't take this personally, as this is part of who he is and we are working on helping him to not be so socially anxious. He is like this with everyone, so it is nothing you did or said. The best way to get him comfortable is to let him approach you. Loud or overly exuberant people scare him, so the more diminutive you can be, the better. Please don't try to hug or kiss him. Don't ask him questions at first, as this puts him on the spot. You can make comments to him, but please don't have an expectation that he should reply back. He may not say please or thank you, but trust me it's not because he is trying to be rude. He is a very polite child at home, but the fear of talking can overwhelm him and prevent him from using his manners. Once he's comfortable with your presence, it might be helpful to sit next to him and do a parallel activity. It might take him several visits to get comfortable. If you haven't seen him in a while, it might seem as if you are starting over with him. This happens when he hasn't been around someone for a while, but give him time and he'll start to get comfortable again. All I ask is that you are patient because I value your relationship with him and I want to help it grow—it will just take some time.*

You might have to remind people periodically of what will help your child, as they may forget or may not realize what behaviors can be overwhelming to your child. Try to discuss these issues out of earshot of your child. Do not put them on the spot or have them perform any cute things they have done at home. If they start to relax and do something funny while in the presence of everyone, do not laugh or point it out to everyone else. Socially cautious children tend to be sensitive to unsolicited attention and will often feel people are laughing *at* them, not *with* them.

In general, it would be beneficial for your child to meet with relatives and friends in a one-to-one setting and not in large numbers. If your child is surrounded by tons of friends and family they will be overwhelmed and consumed with surviving the crowd. If you want to grow individual relationships, you'll have more success setting up individual get togethers.

Inevitably, I am sure you'll have family functions that require you to be around a larger number of family and friends. In these cases, you will have much more success if you show up early. Letting your child acclimatize to the party environment before all the guests have arrived will help them get the lay of the land before they have to contend with a crowd of people. If possible, set up a quiet room or space where your child can play or "reset" if they are feeling overwhelmed. You can bring their favorite toy or coloring book to entertain them when they might need some alone time.

If you are attending a party or a large social gathering, it is wise to not schedule anything right after the event. Social gatherings can be exhausting for children who find social situations stressful. These events will most likely be draining for your child, so plan on going home for some quiet time after a party.

If your child received gifts at the party and was unable to say thank you while you were there, have them record a thank you message you can send after the party. This teaches your child good manners and also lets friends and relatives know that your child was appreciative, but just had a hard time expressing it in that environment.

Working with your relatives and friends on how to approach your child is half the battle. The second part of the equation is working directly with your child. It is hoped that you have set up an optimal social situation (or as optimal as is possible) by prepping your friends and family and giving them pointers on how to approach your child. Now it is time to help prepare your child.

Tell your child exactly what they can expect when they are going to meet someone. Describe how they look or, better still, show them a picture. If they are a relative, explain who they are to your child, "Your uncle is coming over. He is my brother. You know how John is your brother. Well Uncle Tom is my brother." The more your child knows what to expect, the less anxious they will be. Outline exactly what will be happening, "Your uncle is going to come over for lunch. We will then probably talk for a little while and then he'll leave." If your child has a high level of anxiety, prepare them to maybe just smile or say hi before they go off to play on their own. You can tell your child, "I know that you have a hard time talking to people. Uncle Tom loves you and will be happy to see you. Do you think you can just smile at him or tell him hi?" If your child has some strong apprehension about doing these small steps, you might want to encourage them by making it a treasure box challenge where they can earn a prize if they smile or say hi. The purpose of encouraging this behavior isn't to make your brother happy, although that is an added benefit. The goal is to help your child take baby steps in developing a relationship with others, especially those people who will play an important role in their life. As your child learns to warm up to family, it will open the door to deeper and more meaningful connections with relatives in the future.

Playing with others

Younger toddlers typically play next to their peers—this is also known as parallel play. Older toddlers will have brief interactions with their peers. Socially anxious toddlers tend to avoid their peers all together. Toddlers can be unpredictable. They can scratch, bite and hit. They might take your toys from you or push you down. They can suddenly burst out crying or yell in anger. They don't abide by any social rules or norms. For these reasons, the socially anxious toddler would much rather avoid their own kind.

If your child is nervous around their peers they might completely ignore children when they walk past. They won't respond to any questions asked of them by other children. They might grab your leg or shadow you when other kids are present. They might refuse to play on the playground or run around the park if they see other children there. At playdates, they usually hover next to you and ignore your coaxing to go and play. At birthday parties, they refuse to partake in any of the festivities and stay right next to you the entire time. These behaviors can be exhausting, frustrating and sometimes embarrassing for any parent!

How do you help your child become more comfortable around other children? This is a slow process that takes time and patience. Toddlers are not always social to begin with, so the level of comfort will grow as your child develops and gets older. Having said that, you can do some things to help facilitate their level of comfort around other children, even at this stage of development.

For starters, stack the deck in your favor and expose your child to social situations where there are only one or two children at most. Your initial goal is to help your child feel comfortable around children close to their own age. Ideally you would want to find a child who matches your child's temperament as closely as possible. I know this might be a tall order. You are trying to find another child who will remain as quiet and as non-threatening as your child will be. You don't want your child to have to fend off a peer who is grabbing for their toys and pulling their hair. Those situations will naturally come, but for these initial steps, you need a drama-free playdate.

When arranging a playdate, keep it limited to one friend for a while. Tell your child which friend is coming over and what they look like, if they don't know already. Explain to your child how you met their friends. Just like with family visits, you want to detail exactly what will happen at the visit. "Your friend will come over and play with you in the playroom. I will talk to her mommy in the living room. I will make pizza for all of us and you and your friend can sit at your little table together. After that they will probably go home." This helps your child have a good understanding of the sequential order of the visit.

If your child has never had a friend over before, they may be surprised that they are going to have to share their plates, their table and especially their toys with someone else. Explain what sharing is before your playdate. Read books on sharing and taking turns to help solidify the concept in your child's mind. This is especially important if your child is an only child. Only children may have a harder time initially understanding the concept of sharing if they haven't been exposed to any playdates before. If you think this will be a real struggle, have your child pick out the plates and cups for their friend to use prior to the playdate. Tell your child that when kids come to your home, the other child won't have any toys so they will have to share their toys with them. Let your child decide, prior to the playdate, if there are any toys that they do not want to share. Take any toys that are deemed "off limits" by your toddler out of the room. Don't be surprised if your child still has a hard time sharing. This is a preemptive strike, but not a complete fix for toddler possessiveness. To further reduce any possible conflict between toddlers, you can buy a craft activity that is new to both children. Doing a craft together, or another structured activity that requires limited interaction, can minimize stress and make for a successful first visit.

You can help your child develop social skills by playing with them periodically. Try to play with your child the way another child would play with them. Teach them how to share and how to speak up if they do not like how they are being treated. Purposely set up pretend scenarios where your child has to practice speaking up. You can tell them, "I am going to pretend to be a child who doesn't know how to share. Show me what you can do when this happens." You can do puppet shows for your child, showing two children playing and resolving conflict that emerges while they play. When your child is having an actual playdate, you can help script some basic interactions for them; for example, practice saying things like, "What's your name?" and "Do you want to play?" Some children need help learning how to initiate peer interaction. You can tell them that if they are having trouble with someone who is not sharing or who is hurting them, they can come and get you if they need some extra help.

When your child's friend arrives at your home, spend some time with the two children before you focus on the other parent and move on to adult conversation. Sit on the floor and help your child initiate conversation. Ask your child to ask the other child their name. If your child is too reserved to begin the conversation, ask the child yourself. This helps model positive social interactions for your child. Once your child seems somewhat comfortable, let your child play with their friend without you hovering too much. You don't want to be too overbearing.

Your initial goal is just to get your child comfortable being around another child. As time progresses, you will want to remove some of these crutches and have a more natural playdate where there is an opportunity for spontaneous conflict and resolution.

Some socially anxious children are more acutely aware of other children's emotions and distress. Sometimes these children can find other people's distress so stressful they can get overwhelmed themselves. If you see your child staring at another child who is having a strong emotional reaction, help identify the emotion and feeling around the situation. "Are you watching that boy cry? That boy is crying because he doesn't want to leave. Do you sometimes get sad when you have to leave too? Don't worry, he'll be okay." The more you label and process other children's feelings, the more adept your child will become at reading and understanding social cues.

Besides structured playdates, you can teach your child social skills in more natural settings like the park. Initially it might take some doing to just get your child to play next to another child. Frequent exposure to peer interaction at the park will help your child adapt quicker to having other children around. If your child refuses to play, stand near them as they play around other children. Eventually you will want to stand next to them just until they seem more at ease and then sit down and observe them. As with the playdate, you don't want to hover when it is not necessary. Your child will start to depend on your presence and will associate their calmness with you being near them. You do not want your child to make that inadvertent connection, as this will hamper their ability to be socially independent. As children get slightly older and more comfortable, you can offer scripts to your child prior to going to the park. Tell your child to go up to another child and ask, "Do you want to play?" You can set up play challenges telling your child that they can earn a treasure box toy if they are brave and ask another child to play with them. I would not recommend doing this until your child is completely comfortable parallel playing around other children. Remember, toddlers are not developmentally socially advanced and are just developing cooperative play skills. Your average toddler would not naturally go up to another child and ask them to play. It might be good to set up these challenges when your child is almost out of toddlerhood and shows comfort around others.

If your child is invited to birthday parties, do not expect that they will join their friends in the activities. Birthday parties are chaotic, loud and overstimulating. Go to birthday parties early to help your child feel less overwhelmed and give them time to get used to the environment before all the other children show up. Your child will most likely feel uncomfortable and will want to stay close by your side. I wouldn't recommend that you continually pressure your child to join the other kids and leave your side. Let your child know what activities are happening and let them choose if they want to participate. If they don't want to join in, offer to stand with them. If your child still doesn't want to participate, I would leave it alone. You are making progress by just exposing your child to such a chaotic, overstimulating event. I would not recommend avoiding birthday parties for this very reason. The more exposure your child has to these types of situations, the quicker they will acclimatize to these events in the future.

Socially anxious children are sensitive to people looking and laughing at them. Most of the time they are just being self-conscious or paranoid. Explain to your child that people look at other people all the time and that it is normal. Point out how your child stares at other people when they are at the store or at the park. Talk about how people laugh and it doesn't mean they are laughing at them. Point out when people are laughing near them and show them how they are not laughing at them. Tell them that when they are funny, it is normal for other people to think they are cute and laugh with them. Explain how those people are not making fun of them when they think they are funny.

If your child goes to a daycare they might have a hard time being friendly with the other children. You can talk to the director or directly to the teacher and ask if your child could be paired up with another child with a similar temperament. It may be too difficult for your child to find a friend with a similar personality. The teacher can pick out a partner and encourage the friendship by having the children sit together and do activities as a pair.

CHAPTER 9

Anxious Parenting and Fostering Independence

Sharon and Henry

Sharon had a difficult childhood. When Sharon was a young child her father divorced her mother and she never saw him again. She and her sisters were left to live with their mentally unstable mother. Sharon always lived on pins and needles around her mother. She was either invisible around her mom or she was the focus of her mother's rage. She felt rejected and unimportant throughout most of her childhood. She grew up vowing never to be the kind of mother her mom had been to her.

When Sharon had her little girl, Margo, she was determined to give her a better life than she had experienced. Margo had been a frail and sickly infant and Sharon held her baby morning, noon and night. A slight fever or a runny nose could cause Sharon to go into a complete panic. She didn't know what she would do if anything ever happened to Margo. Her husband would try and tell Sharon to relax and enjoy the baby, but Sharon felt he just didn't love Margo the way that she did.

Margo grew into a healthy, active toddler, but Sharon continued to feel she needed to protect her daughter. Sharon had Margo sleep in their bed until she was around two. At two, Henry encouraged his wife to let Margo sleep in her own room. Margo had a hard time separating from her mom and would cry and run into their room. Sharon got angry at Henry for forcing Margo into so much discomfort and she decided she would sleep with Margo in Margo's bed. Sharon would stroke her hair and sing to her as she fell asleep. Henry felt as if he were invisible. He didn't see much of his wife anymore. Sharon had moved some of her clothes into Margo's room where she slept each night.

Sharon's day was consumed with meeting Margo's every whim. She was always right by Margo's side. When Margo insisted on wearing her tights, tutu and ballet slippers and nothing else to the grocery store, Sharon let her, even though it was raining and very cold out. She didn't want to upset Margo and she hated to see her cry. When Margo refused to eat food that got her hands sticky, Sharon would pick up the food for her and put it in her mouth. Henry was concerned that at nearly three years old his daughter wasn't feeding herself most of the time.

Margo didn't like to do things for herself. Potty training went pretty well, but she didn't like to wipe herself. Sharon never attempted to show Margo how to wipe, she just decided she would wipe for her. Henry voiced concern that Sharon wasn't even trying to let her do it herself. "It's okay to help her, but at least give her a chance," he'd tell Sharon. Sharon would grow irate at his parenting advice. "Don't tell me how to parent Margo!" She'd shout.

Sharon didn't like Henry spending time with Margo. She felt Henry didn't know how to handle Margo the way she did. Margo grew very dependent on Sharon. She was used to her mom doing everything for her. Her mom picked out her clothes and put them on her. Margo didn't know how to put her own clothes on and was never shown how. Whenever her dad tried to do anything for her she would scream and cry. To Sharon this was proof that Henry should just leave the parenting up to her.

Henry felt hurt and frustrated by this rejection from both his wife and daughter. He grew resentful of both of them. He felt he had no say in how Margo was being parented.

Margo grew into a very anxious toddler. She was wary of other people. She would hide in her mother's arms. Sharon didn't mind. She thought it was good for Margo not to be so trusting of other people, because after all, trust should be earned. It was also proof of how much Margo loved Sharon. She would readily talk for Margo in those situations. Margo got used to letting her mom talk for her. She would occasionally whisper things to her mom and her mom would relay them to the person trying to talk to Margo.

Sharon felt it was important to teach Margo how to keep herself safe. She talked about germs and how they could make her very sick. She had Margo wash her hands many times a day, just like she did. She told her that bees could sting her and she would hustle her inside whenever she saw one flying by. She told her to be careful on the jungle gym and she did not let her climb parts that she thought looked too scary. When it looked as if Margo was taking too big a risk on the jungle gym, she would remind her that she didn't want to fall and wind up in the hospital. When they went to a festival or to an amusement park, she'd tell Margo to be careful not to get lost. She said if she didn't stay right next to her mom a stranger could take her and she'd never see her again.

Margo would panic if her mom was not in the same room with her. She followed her from room to room. Sharon allowed Margo to shower with her and, if she needed to use the bathroom, she'd just take Margo in with her. Sharon stayed by her side and kept her entertained throughout the day playing dolls, reading books and doing crafts. Margo never played alone and was constantly entertained with well-thought-out craft projects and an endless supply of newly purchased books.

When Henry's mother came by, which was happening less and less, Margo would just ignore her grandmother and would tug at her mom's sleeve to play with her. Her grandma would say,

"Margo, your mommy is trying to talk to me." Sharon would get upset with her mother-in-law and would say that she couldn't expect her to ignore Margo and she would cut their visit short. Margo consumed Sharon's time and she would not allow her to talk on the phone or have any other interactions other than with her. If Sharon tried to talk to her husband, Margo would get in between them, put her hands on her mom's cheeks and pull her cheeks in Margo's direction. "Play with me!" she'd shout at her mom. Her mom would feel guilty during these times and would be angry with herself for ignoring Margo and letting someone else take her attention away from her number one priority—her daughter.

Margo had a hard time playing with other children. She was used to her mom playing the way she wanted them to play. Other children called Margo bossy and Margo would often storm off and have a meltdown when other kids wouldn't do things her way. Sharon would make a note of the children she didn't play well with and would not arrange a playdate with that child again. After all, Margo played fine with her, so something must be wrong with that other child.

Margo was also difficult for anyone who tried to babysit her. She insisted they did everything exactly as her mom did it and if they didn't listen to her, she'd scream and shout. Usually the babysitter had to call Sharon back home early. Inside Sharon felt proud that no one else could take care of her child as well as she could. She also felt it spoke of the intense love that she and Margo had for each other that she wasn't able to function without her.

Margo

Margo loved spending time with her mommy. Her mommy often told her that no one else loved her as much as she did. She also told her that she kept her safe at night while she slept. She was so mad at her daddy for making her sleep in her own room.

Mommy told her that her daddy just didn't understand how much she needed her mommy.

Margo was able to do whatever she wanted. She knew that if she cried, pouted or talked in a baby voice her mommy would feel bad and would give her whatever she wanted. She didn't like to be told no and her mommy didn't like to make her upset. One time her daddy told her to clean up the toys she had dumped in the middle of the living room. She said, "No, I no want to!" Her daddy told her she had to or she'd go into time out. Margo did what she normally did when she was trying to get her parent to change their mind—she cried and pouted. This time, however, instead of getting her way, her daddy put her in time out. She cried so hard she started to gag. Her mommy came home and her mommy and daddy started yelling. Her mommy ran to her, hugged her and apologized for how her daddy treated her. Her mommy started crying. She didn't know what to do. Why was her mommy crying? Had Daddy done something bad? She thought maybe she should stay away from him.

Margo hated the way sticky things felt on her hands and fingers. She loved eating french fries with ketchup, but she hated to get ketchup on her hands. She would complain and say, "You do it!" to her mommy. Her mommy would scoop up a french fry, dip it in ketchup and place it in Margo's mouth. "More!" She'd shout at her mommy. Why should she get her hands dirty? Her mommy could do it for her.

Margo also hated the idea of getting poop on her hands. Gross! She refused to wipe and insisted that her mommy wipe for her. She didn't remember ever having to wipe herself. Now her mommy didn't even ask if she needed help wiping. Margo would just say, "I pooped," and her mommy would grab a wipe and start cleaning her up. Who would wipe her when her mommy wasn't with her? Her daddy said she must try to wipe on her own first. Why did her daddy have to be so mean!

Margo didn't like doing anything that seemed too hard. Taking her pants off seemed too hard, so she would just lie there and her mommy would pull them off her. She would just sit in front of the TV watching cartoons as her mommy pulled and tugged at her arms and legs and got her into a new outfit for the day. She would sometimes yell at her mommy that she couldn't see the TV. Her mommy would apologize and move out of her way.

Her mommy warned her that she shouldn't talk to other people. She told her that some people were bad and some people could hurt her. Why would people hurt her? When strangers would try to talk to her, she could feel her mommy holding her closer. She was too afraid to talk to them. Her mommy would happily talk for her. Sometimes Margo whispered what she wanted her mom to say to people. She even did this to people she should feel comfortable around, like her grandma, aunts and uncles.

Margo's mommy wanted to keep her safe so she told her all about the things that could hurt her. She knew about germs—they were invisible and could make her very sick. She had to wash the invisible germs off her hands many times a day. Sometimes she'd look down at her hands and wonder if any germs had crept back on her hands. She knew bees could sting her and that she could get very sick and wind up at the hospital. Her mommy got very scared of bees, so that made her extra fearful! She also knew that she should be careful when playing on the playground. Her mommy said she could fall and crack her head open. What would her head look like if it was cracked open? She didn't want to find out! When they were in a crowd of people, her mommy told her to stay near her and not get lost. She said if she got lost her mommy may never see her again. That was the scariest thing she had ever heard. From then on she insisted on being carried most of the time. There sure were a lot of dangers everywhere!

When her mommy talked to other people that made her very angry. That was her mommy and she didn't like sharing her with anyone. Margo got bored on her own and she liked it when her mommy played with her. When her grandma came to visit, she would take her mommy's attention away from her. This made Margo mad and she would pull at her mommy's sleeve to get *her attention. Her mommy usually said she was sorry. She knew she should only pay attention to her.*

Margo preferred not to play with other kids. They never listened to her like her mommy did! They wanted to do things their way, not her way! She would tell them what to say when they were playing with dolls and they didn't listen to her. Her mommy always listened. She had a meltdown, but usually the other kid wouldn't even say sorry. It was no fun playing with kids!

Margo hated it when other people came to babysit her. Why did her mommy leave her? The babysitters didn't know how to do things the right way. When she corrected them they would tell her she was not in charge. She thought to herself, "I'm going to tell my mommy on you!" If they were really mean to her she would cry and cry until she knew they would get fed up and call her mommy. Her mommy always hugged her and apologized for leaving.

Margo didn't want to go to school. School sounded scary. There were no mommies at school to help her with all the things she needed help doing. What would she do if she needed to take her coat off? What would she do if she needed to go poop and no one was there to wipe her? She didn't want to play with other kids. She didn't want to talk to a teacher. They wouldn't love her the way her mommy loved her.

Nature versus nurture

As we discussed at the beginning of this book, much of your young child's personality and temperament is part of the way they were born. Having a child with an anxious predisposition has a strong genetic component and does not necessarily have anything to do with your parenting. Having said that, there are environments that can nurture *in*dependence and strength coping mechanisms and there are environments that can nurture *de*pendence and reinforce fears. Although your child may have an anxious personality, how they adapt and cope with that anxiety is up to you and how you parent them.

I have worked with many parents who understand their child's anxiety from their own personal experiences. Due to these experiences, the parents know first-hand how debilitating anxiety can be and want to arm their child with coping mechanisms that they may not have had themselves as children. I have also worked with parents who have never got a complete handle on their own anxiety. They may not recognize that they even have anxiety and they may make excuses and other rationalities for their anxious belief systems. They may even incorporate their anxiety into how they parent, becoming an anxious, nervous parent.

Children develop their understanding of the world through the eyes of their parents. When parents hover over their child, they convey a message to that child that they are not safe. When parents do everything for their child, they are sending a message that they don't believe their child could do it for themselves. For a child who is not pre-wired to be anxious, this type of parenting may have limited effects on the child. For an anxious child, this type of anxious parenting can unintentionally create the perfect storm of reinforcing nature and further nurturing anxiety within their child.

There are parents with their own phobias and compulsions who externally instill those fears into their children. They point out germs and the lurking dangers that exist throughout their day. They might make their child excessively wash their hands, their toys or their clothes. They might make them change their outfit if they have been outside the house, or show their child their own intense fears over bugs and bees. They might hover over their child while they eat and constantly make micromanaging comments like, "Chew more before you swallow. Take smaller bites. Don't choke." For a child who is predisposed to become anxious, this type of parenting will be the tripwire for that genetic seed that rests inside the child.

Childhood scars

Besides sharing their child's genetic predisposition for anxiety, some parents are carrying residual emotional baggage from their own childhood. If you are parenting from guilt or fear, this may be based on your own childhood experiences. I have worked with many parents who have told me, "I just didn't want to be anything like my parents." Unfortunately for some parents, they go to the opposite extreme, creating dependent and over-protected children. They want to be there for their children to such a degree that they unintentionally become overbearing and do everything *for* their child. They fear disciplining, as their own childhood had intense discipline. They fear letting their child fall and recover, as they fell and no one was there to pick them up.

What they are unable to see is that there is a healthy side to discipline and independence that was not modeled for them. Anxious children need to have clear boundaries set for them and they need to fall and pick themselves up in order to gain confidence and a feeling of self-sufficiency. Letting your child make mistakes is not letting your child suffer, but rather letting them learn the feeling of fighting for success. This can be a hard and painful approach to parenting. It is much easier to be right under your child with a safety net, protecting them from obvious mistakes and smoothing the road ahead of them, so they feel no bumps. The anxious child, more so than any other child, needs to learn how to handle those bumps and they need to be taught how to navigate through them, not around them.

If you felt ignored and unimportant growing up, you might revel in the feeling of being needed by your baby. Sometimes this need to be needed can turn into an unhealthy desire to keep your child from turning into an independent toddler. You might fear losing your baby and subsequently the important role you play in their life. It might be scary when your once clingy baby runs in the opposite direction and never looks back. You might feel uncomfortable seeing your baby grow up and you therefore let them carry their blanket around in public or still enjoy giving them a bottle when they are almost out of toddlerhood. The important thing to remember is that your child, no matter what age, will always need you. Children will always seek out the support and understanding of loving parents.

Not every person who has had a difficult childhood grows up to have parenting issues. Many adults who have had very abusive or traumatic upbringings, evolve into the most balanced and understanding parents *because* of their experiences. Other parents may have worked out their issues in therapy long before they ever had children. If you feel you have unresolved issues that make you parent out of guilt or because of your own needs, you might want to seek a few sessions with a therapist.

Some parents have spouses who trigger bad memories from their childhood. Their spouse can be too stern or too strict for their comfort and it may remind them of a parent they had difficulties with in their own childhood. They may feel guilty that their child has to have a parent like they did growing up. To counterbalance their spouse's strict disposition, these parents might try to comfort their child by undermining their spouse and undoing their discipline. This a confusing message to the anxious toddler, who can't handle mixed messages and needs clear boundaries and rules to follow. This also, inevitably, causes friction in the marriage and can cause ongoing conflict in the home.

Fostering independence

Even if you know where your anxious parenting comes from, you may be at a loss as to how to foster independence and confidence in your toddler. Parenting styles are pretty ingrained and it takes a conscious effort to bring about significant change. Some parents will fiercely defend their parenting approach and will deny that it stems from their own anxieties or childhood. Changing your parenting style can feel uncomfortable and scary. You might worry it will upset your child or that your child won't like you if you change the way you approach them. Knowing you want to make a concerted effort to grow your child's confidence and self-efficacy is the first step.

Fostering independence does not mean ignoring your child. It takes just as much energy and involvement to create an independent and confident child as it does to create a dependent, over-protected one. You want to start letting your child do things for themselves, whenever they show signs they are ready. During the toddler phase their abilities can be ever-changing, and what your child is unable to do one day, they can sometimes be capable of doing the next. You have to constantly reassess—can my child do this for themselves? If the answer is yes, you may do it for them anyway because:

> they take too much time
> they don't do it perfectly
> they might spill something
> they might not get it on right
> it is too hard for them
> they might get frustrated
> they might fail
> they might grow up.

However, put your worries aside and let them try anyway. Things typically do not go smoothly when a toddler is doing it themselves. Stand next to them and encourage them. When they mess up, tell them it is alright and they should try again. If they insist you do it for them, tell them you know they can do it. If they start to cry and get frustrated, do the first few steps for them. Always allow them to finish the task themselves, even if it is just the final snap or pull through of a pant leg. You want them to feel the accomplishment of doing it themselves in the end. When they do it, even if it is that small, last step, praise them and tell them, "I knew you could do it!" This helps to develop their level of motivation and will improve their ability to keep moving forward, without giving up. If they want to be your helper, but the task is beyond their abilities, give them an alternate task to do. "You can't cut the apple, the knife is too sharp, but you can put the peels in the garbage for me."

When your child needs help, try not to swoop in quickly and "fix" the problem for them. If possible, verbally support them. For instance, if your child is having a hard time getting a cap off, a verbal direction might be something like, "Twist the cap, don't pull it." Give them a visual cue by showing them with your hands how to twist. If at all possible, do not take the challenge away from them by completing it yourself. You want to let your child know it is alright to ask for help, but you do not want to send a message that it means you will do it for them. This can be a balancing act of helping your child, while fostering their independence. When you do things completely for your child you are reconfirming to them that they are incapable of doing it without your help.

If you are showing your child how to do something for the first time, have them do it as you show them. For instance, if you are doing an art project, set up a spot for you and a spot for your child. Have your child follow your steps as you go. If they get stuck, show them how to do it on your example, not on their work. You can also work on things together to instill the concept of teamwork. You just have to be aware of limiting your involvement and be conscious of taking a step back to let your child do most of it.

Obviously, life is busy and hectic and you cannot always let your child do things for themselves, that's completely understandable. Every parent does things for their child due to time constraints or their level of frustration on that particular day. It is just good to be aware that when you have the time and patience, encouraging your child to work through their own problems helps them develop lifelong problem-solving skills.

Another way to foster independence is to encourage your child to start making some small choices for themselves. If you have an older toddler, one almost out of toddlerhood, you can start to encourage them to pick out their own clothes. You can pair up various outfits and put them in bins or in a shoe organizer that hangs from their closet. In each bin or hole you can put a complete outfit. This gives your child the freedom to choose their clothes without the burden of knowing what matches. When your child is older, you can have bins of pants that are color coded to match bins of shirts. For example, you could have a yellow bin of pants and a yellow bin of shirts that match interchangeably. You might have several color-coded bins or you might just rotate what clothes you have in the bins, making sure they all match with each other. Toddlers typically like to exert their own style and like making their own choices at this stage of development. If your toddler finds picking out their own clothes overwhelming, wait until they are a little bit older.

Independent play

Teaching your child how to play independently is an invaluable lesson that helps them to be creative and use their own active imagination. When they play alone or with their siblings, they learn how to maintain and extend their own entertainment without an adult constantly facilitating and orchestrating that for them. Children who are unable to play independently become overly dependent on others to create entertainment for them. They are also at risk of struggling in school due to their inability to work and play on their own.

Some parents feel that they are bad parents if they are not engaged in play with their child every minute of the day. As with everything, balance is key. Yes, it is fun to get on the floor and play with your child. This is a wonderful bonding experience, but teaching your child the skills of independent play is also crucial, especially as your toddler gets older and is closer to pre-school age. You do not have to have a planned craft activity, a cool science project or a well-scripted tea party arranged to keep every minute of the day stimulating and entertaining for your child. It is nice for children to learn how to cope with down time. When your child has time to be bored, they have time to initiate their own creativity. Letting your child develop their own creativity will be helpful in all areas of their life. A key coping mechanism to ward off anxiety in older children is distraction. When children are anxious, down time can cause an increase in negative thoughts. If you teach your child at a young age how to limit their down time by growing their imagination and learning to develop their own entertainment, they will be well armed with distraction techniques when they are a little bit older.

Some parents might say, "I would love my child to play independently, but they follow me around all day begging me to play with them." Of course your child would love you to be their best friend and playmate throughout their day—after all, they are not in school full time and don't have playmates readily available. Setting limits and having your child play without you several times a day will give your child the space to build up their own play skills. It will also teach them how to work independently—a crucial skill they will need to be successful in school. Your child will not have the full, undivided attention of their teacher when they are in a school environment, and as your child gets closer to pre-school age, it is important to start giving them the skills to cope without an adult's constant attention.

Having your child play independently does not mean you have to ignore your child. Rather, it means periodically setting up play situations for your child and then allowing them time and space to play alone or with their siblings. They can play in the same room to you. Independent play is more about who is engaged in the play rather than how close in proximity your child is to you. In general, it is nice to have your toddler playing around you, so you can periodically observe their play and gain insights into their play themes. When your child makes up their own stories in their fantasy play, they are giving you a little window into what's on their mind and what themes and problems they are grappling with in real life. Remember, play themes are much exaggerated and it is important to not take their play too literally, as it is often more symbolic in nature.

So, you might be on board with teaching independent play skills, but still at a loss as to how to make that happen. This approach is centered on the older toddler who should be able to start playing independently. For starters, you have to set clear limits with your child. Specify when you are playing with them and when you are not. Do not set a pattern of giving in when your child begs you repeatedly to play with them. In general, giving in to your child's nagging is not good parenting protocol. You do not want to send a message to your child that "no" really means "just beg more."

The more organized your child's toys are, the longer and more effectively they will play. Anxious children can get easily overwhelmed in chaotic and unstructured environments. Having toys placed individually on low shelves lets your child see what toys are available. Putting toys like LEGO®, cars and trains in bins, sorted by category, helps simplify play. The more organized and simplified the toys are, the more engaged your child will be. You can divide your child's toys into groups and have only one grouping out at a time. Take the other groups of toys and place them in your garage, and rotate what toys are offered to your child. This creates refreshed excitement periodically and helps to re-engage your child's interest in their toys. If your child's toys and playroom remain messy, their play is more likely to be disorganized and brief.

Have shelves and drawers throughout the house strategically filled with children's activities. What you place in these nooks and crannies will depend on your child's level of maturity and your level of trust with them accessing what you leave in the drawers. In the kitchen, have one drawer full of small, pretend pots and pans that they can access. In your pantry, have a small broom and brush for them to freely use. If you have the space, have a small table and chairs in the kitchen, where your child can do activities and have their snacks without your assistance. If you have an entertainment center with low drawers, you can fill them with puzzles or sorting materials. If you have a drawer in your coffee table, you can place paper, coloring books and crayons for your child to color in there. Fill a craft cart with various craft materials you are comfortable with your toddler accessing independently, and place stickers and paper in a drawer for them to take out. If you are comfortable, you can have a bin of play dough and a bin of cookie cutters accessible. You can have a bin filled with containers of squishy sand and sandcastle molds. You can make a closet (if you have the space) into a dress-up room, with low-placed battery-operated lights. Put dress-up clothes on hooks and put a child's mirror at a low level in the closet for them to look at themselves. You can have a drawer that is just for your child's treasures. If you have a house with tile or wood floors, and you don't mind, you can have small scooters that your child can ride around on in the house. If your child has a playroom, organize their play area according to theme. If your child has a pretend kitchen, once in a while organize it and put all the food away. If your child has babies, put all the baby doll items in one bin or place them in the cribs. An organized area will hold your child's attention longer.

If your child is struggling with what to play with or seems to be aimlessly walking around bored, direct them in their play. You can tell them, "I think your babies are hungry. Do you think you should feed them?" or "I wonder which one of your cars is the fastest. Maybe your cars want to race?" If they are not open to subtle suggestions, you can start naming accessible projects for them to start. "Why don't you go get some stickers and make some sticker art on paper?"

Periodically set up adult-directed activities and then let your child work on the project alone. Structuring a few independent projects throughout the day will help break up the monotony of unstructured play and will give the child some space from parent–child play. If you have your own work or projects, sit next to your child as you both engage in your own individual work. Below is a list of projects that can independently entertain older toddlers:

> stickers on paper
> contact paper—stick anything on it (great for putting little shiny treasures on)
> coloring
> play dough
> treasure hunt (hide items and then let your child roam around finding them)
> stamp art
> dot art (use bingo markers—these can be bought from art stores and are often machine washable)
> slime play (homemade recipes are easy to find online)
> whipped cream with food coloring for finger painting
> kinetic sand and sandcastle molds
> rainbow bread (use a plastic medicine dropper and water with food coloring to color white bread)

> baking soda and dyed white vinegar (when the child mixes white vinegar and food coloring with baking soda it reacts and foams up)

> bucket of animals or dinosaurs

> dinosaurs inside jello (fun to dig out and play with at the same time)

> dress-up

> doll play

> doctor kit with real bandaids.

Set healthy boundaries

It's never to early to start establishing healthy boundaries, especially for the anxious child who may have a harder time with limits. Often, parents will not start to set limits until a child is older and already set in their ways. Boundaries may not be respected and limits may have to be reminded, but at least the seeds are being planted. It is important for older toddlers to understand that parents and other adults have priorities besides them. Parents can help their child develop patience and improve delayed gratification if they do not jump every time their child needs or wants something. If you are in the middle of doing something and your three-year-old demands a snack, it is alright to tell them, "Mommy is doing something right now. I will get it for you in just one minute." This helps your child understand that they will not always get everything instantly and will sometimes have to be patient.

You might be used to waiting on your child hand and foot, but as they get older it becomes less about what they cannot do and more about what they just don't want to do. If you have an older toddler and they are sitting on the couch playing and they want you to go get their water cup for them (and you are nowhere near it!), it is helpful to encourage them to go and get it themselves. This is not because you are lazy or you don't want to attend to your child's needs, but rather because you are starting to teach your child that they are capable of meeting their own basic needs. You can explain to your child, "I am sitting down too. We are both comfortable right now. Is it fair that I should get up to get you your cup? We are both far away from your cup. Do I want your cup or do you want it?" This helps your child realize that you are human too and teaches them how to be empathetic and less demanding of others. Over time, your child will notice when you do something considerate or unnecessary for them and there will be a greater level of appreciation and gratitude. You will also find that your child might surprise you by reciprocating acts of helpfulness and kindness!

It is normal for parents to have other household responsibilities during the day besides watching their children. Many parents live in perpetual guilt. You feel guilty if you are playing with your children and not cleaning the house. You feel guilty if you are cleaning the house and not playing with your children. It seems as if you can't win as a parent! If you have an anxious toddler who follows you around the house, stopping all other activities and being consumed with them does not help your child in the long run. It is important for them to realize that parents have other responsibilities and you do not want to reinforce their anxious behavior with further attention. Give your child their own toy vacuum, mop or rag to help you do household chores. Some children love this, which is no surprise since at this age they spend most of their play time copying you anyway! If you are doing laundry, have your child help you by handing you the clothes. If you are cooking, give them something to mix or have them play with their own dishes and fake food. If you are doing dishes, have them help you put their plastic dishes away. It might make doing chores slightly longer, but it is time well spent.

When you are talking to another adult, it is helpful to teach your child patience and the ability to handle delayed responses.

Anxious children might have less patience and might feel a false urgency to tell you something. They might also crave constant attention and may not care that you are talking with someone else. When your child enters pre-school, they will have to wait patiently when a teacher is talking to another student or parent. Teaching your child these boundaries when they are around three will help them cope in the future with delayed responses. Your child will learn to become less anxious when someone cannot answer them right away because you have taught them that delayed responses happen and that their needs are always eventually met.

Anxious children often have a hard time seeing the big picture when they have something to say or something they want to do. They have a feeling of false urgency and want their needs met immediately. You can help your child by teaching them at a young age that, although they want to be listened to right away, they need to respect what is happening around them. It is good to help your child learn that parents are sometimes having other discussions or are sometimes in the middle of other activities. This will help your child adapt in other environments, as other people will not be as attentive as you. This will also enable your child to develop social awareness and consideration of others—all wonderful attributes to foster and grow!

Don't be upset or disappointed if your child continues to interrupt your conversations or remains demanding regardless of your efforts to teach them patience. Teaching toddlers is very much like planting seeds. You do a lot of work planting and watering before you get to see the first sprouts of all your work. The important thing is that you are planting the seeds and are not haphazardly reinforcing negative behavior.

Encourage other relationships

Toddlers with an anxious disposition have a harder time forging close relationships with people outside their family. Anxious toddlers tend to be more cautious and less trusting of those around them. As parents you can help your child work through this by promoting other relationships.

Sometimes this issue starts at home. Anxious toddlers might be more attached to one parent and refuse to let the other parent do anything for them. Some parents will acquiesce and accommodate their child's parental preferences. By not helping your child get out of their comfort zone, you continue to enable this imbalanced relationship. Instead, slowly have the other parent take over some parental responsibilities— not just when the other parent is out or unavailable. If you normally do bath time, have your spouse do bath time once in a while. If your child has a strong reaction to the change, make adjustments to your routine one step at a time. Once your child is used to the other parent taking on some new responsibilities, continue to rotate responsibilities. This helps them develop and maintain authentic relationships with both parents.

Encourage your child to develop close relationships with other family members, if possible. Arrange playdates with just grandma and your child. Let them have their own special time when you are not present. This lets your child attach to other important people in their life. The more supportive relationships your child has the better!

······

CHAPTER 10

• • • • • • • • • • • • • • •

Separation Anxiety

Chloe and Xander

Chloe and Xander always joked about how Alexis had been their easiest child. However, when Alexis turned two, she started to have major issues with separating from her mom. Alexis followed her mom all over the house. Chloe realized that recently there hadn't been a time that Alexis wasn't right under her feet. If Chloe went to the bathroom, Alexis was by the door, crying for her to come out. When Chloe went upstairs, she saw Alexis trotting up behind her.

The issue became further complicated when her dad tried to watch Alexis. Chloe usually worked two nights a week and previously Alexis had had no problem staying at home with her dad. Recently, however, Alexis would scream and cry when her mom was leaving to go to work. Xander tried to not be offended by his daughter's sudden dislike for him, but it was hard to not take it personally. Often Chloe would get so worried about Alexis that she would decide to not go to work and would call in sick.

Xander and Chloe had a date night once a month. They had had the same babysitter since Alexis was born. Everyone was stumped as to why Alexis suddenly started screaming and crying when they tried to leave her. They started to cancel their monthly dates, as it was becoming too stressful to leave Alexis.

Xander and Chloe were at a loss for what to do. Their other two children hadn't gone through an intense period of separation anxiety. They knew it was normal for some kids to go through a period of clinginess, but this seemed extreme!

Alexis

When Alexis turned two, she started noticing when her mom was not in the same room with her. She felt safe when she was near her mom and got nervous when she couldn't see her. Often Alexis would be playing with her toys and would look up to find her mom gone! This was scary for her because she didn't know where her mom was or when she would come back. To avoid this scary feeling, Alexis decided it was just safer to follow her mom around the house. She would watch her mom diligently throughout her day. When she saw her mom preparing to leave the room, she'd grab her blanket and would be right behind her. It made her very upset when her mom wouldn't let her come into the bathroom with her. She'd cry for her mom and her mom would tell her she'd be right there.

Alexis didn't like to be with anyone other than her mom. Her mom took care of her the most and she was used to how she did things. When her mom left her with her dad she didn't know when her mom was coming back. She worried her mom might never come back! She went to a place called "work," but Alexis didn't know what work was or if people came back from it. She loved playing with her daddy, but she worried so much about not being able to see her mom. She would cry until her dad put her mom on the phone. Hearing her mom's voice made her so sad. She missed her so much. She would cry and beg for her mom to come back home, and usually she did.

Alexis loved her babysitter, but when her babysitter arrived, her parents always left. Now she worried about both her mom and dad! She didn't like it when she couldn't see them. Sometimes she'd be playing with her babysitter and they would sneak out when she wasn't keeping a close eye on them. This upset her *greatly and made her want to be more vigilant next time. When the babysitter came again, she clung to her mom's leg so she couldn't disappear like last time. This made it even harder for her parents to leave. Luckily the babysitter came less and less and eventually stopped coming altogether.*

Origins of separation anxiety

Separation anxiety is a normal developmental stage. Usually at around eight to ten months old, children develop an understanding that objects and people still exist when they cannot see them. This knowledge can sometimes bring on an initial bout of separation anxiety. Some children develop a secondary period of separation anxiety at around 12 to 24 months of age. Separation anxiety can come on suddenly and at various ages depending on the child. With most children, it is a healthy, normal phase of development that they pass through with few or no issues. Anxious children are more at risk of developing ongoing separation anxiety so it is important that parents make an effort to help their child develop coping mechanisms as they go through this stage.

As in the vignette at the beginning of this chapter, separation anxiety causes children always to be near their parents, often primarily their mother. They will follow their parent around and will go into panic mode when they are separated. Children with a more intense level of separation anxiety will panic even if their parent leaves the room. Other children might only panic when they are left with another caregiver.

Shadowing behavior at home

When your little one becomes your perpetual shadow, they may be experiencing angst about being separated from you. Children shadow their parents for two different reasons, as we discussed in Chapter 7. The first reason has more to do with the fears they have around them. These children do not want to be alone, but they are comforted as long as someone is in the room with them. The second reason has more to do with the attachment of the parent and child. These children worry excessively about their safety or their mother's safety when they are separated. Although the origin of the behavior is vastly different, the approach to helping your child is similar. You can help your child by reinforcing the concept that *what is gone will reappear*. We discussed some of these approaches in Chapter 7, but we will revisit some of those ideas here.

Games like peek-a-boo are a good place to start with a younger toddler. As your child gets older, Hide and Go Seek is a perfect game to instill positive separation. Keep the game to one room initially and do not make your hiding spots difficult for your child. As they gain more confidence, move the game to two rooms and add rooms as your child's level of anxiety is reduced. Once your child can play Hide and Go Seek without fear, introduce a scavenger hunt game. You can hide objects in one or two rooms and have your child go and look for them. This will motivate your child to go into rooms without you and will allow them to experience the separation without panic. Another fun game is walkie talkie play. This will depend on your child's ability to get the concept of pressing a button to talk, so it is not developmentally appropriate for every toddler. You can go into different rooms and talk to each other. If walkie talkies are too difficult, another option is to use a baby monitor with a camera and talk mode. You can tell your child to go in their room and do something funny and you will tell them what they did—take turns doing this. This is another game that encourages separation, while still being connected and having fun.

Besides playing games, you can help reduce your child's level of hypervigilance by making it a habit always to tell your child where you are going in the house. For instance, if you are going to go upstairs and your child is in the living room, tell them, "I am going upstairs to get the laundry, I will be back down in a minute." Even if you know your toddler is going to be right behind you, telling them your intentions before you leave will reduce their general anxiety over where you are in the house. Your child will eventually learn that mommy tells them when she leaves, so they don't have to keep a close eye on her. In time, your child's level of separation anxiety will be reduced and you will not need to continue telling them where you are going when you are at home.

If you have an older toddler, try to close the door when you are going to the bathroom. Talk to your child through the door to let them know you will be out in a minute. If your child gets nervous, tell them they can put their fingers under the door and you can let them know when you see them. This helps make them feel connected. It is important to close the door when you are going to the bathroom because your older toddler might be going to pre-school in the near future and you want to start establishing the concept of privacy around bathroom activities.

As your toddler gets more comfortable with playing games that improve their separation abilities, try to take separation one step further. Set your child up with an activity and tell them you will be doing a chore in the next room. Your child might come back and check on you, but gently prompt them to go back and work on their activity. By structuring activities in different rooms, you teach your child that they are still safe when you are not right next to them.

Many toddlers will have an object, be it a blanket or stuffed animal, that brings them comfort. This is often referred to as a transitional object and it can provide additional solace in the absence of a parent. If your child doesn't have a transitional object, you could try to develop one by soothing them while having a small blanket in your arms. When your child gets hurt, have the blanket with you as you hold them. Children will make an association between the parental comfort they receive and the blanket. Blankets and stuffed animals can be especially helpful during bedtime and during separations.

Going out

It is important that you get time alone with your spouse. Separation anxiety can be a major barrier to date nights. Even if your child is going through acute separation anxiety, it is helpful and healthy for your child to spend time periodically with another trusted caregiver. When you go out every now and then, you teach your child that you always return and that temporary separation is nothing to panic about.

If your child is going through a difficult period of separation anxiety, it is better to let them get to know their babysitter before you leave them alone for an extended period of time. Have the babysitter spend time with your child without you leaving. This gives your child an opportunity to become friendly with the babysitter without the fear or experience of you leaving.

Once your child is familiar and comfortable with the babysitter, arrange a short outing where you will be back within an hour or two. Go several short outings before you use the babysitter for a full evening out. This gives your child several positive experiences with the caregiver before they are left for a longer period of time. Let your child know ahead of time that you are planning on going out and returning. Speak in a matter-of-fact tone and do not over-verbalize or process this event. "Carol, the babysitter, is coming to watch you for a little while. Mommy and Daddy are going to spend grown-up time together at a restaurant and then we will be back to tuck you up in bed." Be sure to add when you are returning. Since toddlers have no sense of time, use an *activity* to anchor the return, not a specific *time*.

To create an optimal experience for your child, buy or set up a new project the babysitter and your child can do together while you are gone. The more enthralled and entertained your child feels, the less likely it is that they will be focused on your absence. Do not sneak out of the house when you are getting ready to leave. This will just instill panic in your child and will make them more nervous the next time the babysitter shows up. Have the babysitter engage your child in an activity away from the door you will be exiting. Once they are engrossed in that activity, say goodbye to your child. Be brief with your goodbyes and leave as quickly as you can. Have a cute goodbye ritual that has a beginning and end, such as two kisses and then one blown kiss for your child to catch for good luck. If your child cries, let the babysitter calm them down. If you struggle leaving or you come back because you hear your child crying, they will have more intense behaviors the next time you plan on going out. Your behavior will communicate to your child that you are just as nervous as they are and you will validate their fears. Rather, you want to instill a feeling of confidence in your child. You want them to get the message that they are safe in the care of the babysitter and that you leaving for a few short hours is not a big deal.

Try to avoid talking to your child while you are out. If you call the babysitter, ask her not to let your child know you are talking to her. When you talk to your child over the phone, you bring to the surface all those sad emotions that they were just able to move past. Do not stray from the time you told your child you would be home. You are trying to build their trust during this stage and you do not want them to develop mistrust for what you tell them. Although they do not know time, they do know what activity you told them they would be doing when you would return. If you are not sure what time you will return, tell your child that they will be watching a particular TV show or they will be playing a certain game when you get back. Call the babysitter when you are on your way home so she can begin the activity that will alert your child that you are on your way home. When you return, be calm and matter of fact. If you come in throwing your arms around your child as if you thought you'd never see them again, it is going to convey the wrong message!

Daycare

Dropping your child off at daycare can be difficult during a period of separation anxiety. Just remember, no matter what you do, your child is going to cry when you drop them off. The majority of toddlers cry for a brief period of time after they are left and are able to go on to have a fun, productive day.

Visit the daycare several times before you begin your routine of leaving your child at the center. Let them know that you are just going to visit the daycare and meet the teachers and children. When you are ready to have them start daycare, tell them specifically what will be happening that day. "Today we are going to daycare and I am going to help you hang up your coat and sit in the circle with your friends. I am then going to leave like all the other mommies and daddies. After snack time I will come back and pick you up so we can go home." Even though your child will protest and will more than likely cry, it is better to prepare them ahead of time than for them to be caught off guard.

Toddlers do better when they are handed over to another caring adult. Make sure you find a daycare that has nurturing, caring teachers who are willing to hold your child and comfort them when you leave. Bring your child's blanket or stuffed animal and keep it with their other things. Some children like to periodically vistit their blanket or animal for comfort. These brief "resets" can help calm your child throughout the day. Every daycare has their own rules regarding bringing items from home, so talk to the center about their particular policies before your child starts. Most daycares allow your child to keep their blanket or stuffed animal with their other items.

When it is time to leave, have a brief goodbye ritual. As we said earlier, having a cute goodbye routine with a beginning and an end helps keep the goodbye brief. You can do a kiss and a high-five or a kiss in each hand. Once your child is in the arms of the teacher, make a swift exit, but do not sneak out. Do not draw out your goodbyes or try continually to comfort your child. They won't be able to move past the goodbye until you actually leave. Once you leave, do not return to the room, no matter how tempting it may be. When you linger in the room or at the door your child senses your nervousness and will have a harder time settling down. If you are worried, call the center an hour after you leave to get reassurance that your child is doing well.

Although this may seem counterintuitive, do not volunteer or come back and visit during lunch while your child is going through separation anxiety. Every time your child sees you they have to "reset" and readjust to you leaving. Having your child go through several goodbyes throughout their day is not helpful and can negatively impact their ability to adjust to the daycare environment.

• • • • • • • • • • • • • • •

CHAPTER 11

What Are Sensory Issues?

Emily and Jack

Emily and Jack struggled with their son Ryan. He seemed to complain non-stop and always needed things his way. He refused to wear almost anything they bought for him. Emily got frustrated over how much money they spent trying to find clothes that Ryan would agree to wear. He hated jeans and if he had it his way, he would be in his underwear most of the time. When he had to put on bottoms, he preferred cotton shorts, even when it was very cold outside. He hated socks with seams, and Emily and Jack bought him five different brands of socks before they found one he would agree to wear. He had similar issues with shoes. Ryan would love the shoes when he tried them on in the store, but a few days later he would rip them off his feet and refuse to wear them ever again. This would enrage Jack, who felt Ryan was becoming very entitled and spoiled. Ryan preferred to wear crocs or flip flops, even in the winter.

To say Ryan was a picky eater was an understatement. He would eat five foods on a consistent basis, which included: mac-n-cheese, chicken nuggets, pizza, eggs and waffles. He wouldn't try anything new and he insisted that he had the same brand of food each time.

Ryan had an acute sense of hearing and he knew when the garbage truck was coming before his parents could figure out why he was crying and hiding. He covered his ears when his mom vacuumed and he would scream when she turned on the garbage disposal. They learned early on that Ryan was terrified of fireworks and last year they decided not to even go. They felt frustrated with Ryan and didn't know why he was showing such difficult behavior.

Ryan

Ryan felt, smelled and heard everything more intensely than other children. Clothes often felt itchy and painful on his skin. He would try and wear the clothes his parents put on him, but eventually he couldn't take the scratchy, itchy feeling and had to rip them off. He hated his parents getting so mad. Some socks felt as if there was a huge bump at the top of his toe. These bumps would hit against his shoes as he walked and they drove him crazy. How could anyone stand having something that felt like a rock in their shoe all day? His dad would shout at him, "You're fine!" but he didn't feel fine in those socks. Sometimes he would try a pair of shoes on at the store and they would feel really good. He once wanted these super hero shoes so bad that he convinced himself they felt alright. A few days later his feet throbbed all over. The shoes were too tight on the sides and he knew he couldn't wear them anymore. His dad called him spoiled. He didn't know what that meant, but he had a feeling it wasn't a nice word. He cried for the next few days. His parents kept asking him why he was crying. He couldn't tell them it was because he missed his super hero shoes.

His mouth was very sensitive too. He could tell the difference between McDonald's chicken nuggets and Wendy's chicken nuggets. His parents insisted they were the same. He would only eat the ones from McDonald's; he liked the way they felt in his mouth better. His parents called him picky. He didn't pick his food. He didn't like food with bumps or surprises. Some flavors made him feel sick, so he just stuck with the foods he knew he liked.

He wondered why no one else heard what he heard. He hated the low grumble of the angry garbage truck. When he heard those high-pitched breaks, he would hide. When he told his mom it was because of the garbage truck she'd always say, "What truck?" Could she not hear it? He wished that she would warn him when she was going to turn on the garbage disposal. The sudden loud noise made his heart beat so loudly in his ears.

Ryan felt as if he was always disappointing his parents and constantly getting yelled at for things he did not understand. He tried to be a good kid and a good listener, but there were some things he couldn't control. He wished he knew how to explain that to his parents.

What is Sensory Processing Disorder?

There is a close relationship between anxiety and Sensory Processing Disorder (SPD). Children who are struggling with anxiety are much more likely to have sensory processing issues as well. Since sensory issues can be a common component of anxiety, it is key that you have at least a brief understanding of the signs and symptoms of SPD (previously called Sensory Integration Dysfunction). There are entire books solely devoted to the topic of SPD and you should seek out those resources if you want to dive further into the area or want to learn techniques to help your child with SPD.

Put very simply, SPD means the brain has difficulty processing messages to the senses. This makes children either over- or understimulated by sensory input. You can have a child who might be over-reactive (hypersensitive) to smells and noises and yet they might be under-reactive (hyposensitive) to pain and touch. Being over- or under-reactive are not mutually exclusive issues and many children struggle with both.

If you are like many of the parents I work with, you might be at a complete loss to know what I am talking about. Although knowledge of SPD is becoming more common, it still remains more of a mystery than other childhood issues. Let's look at the different areas of sensory processing and the struggles a child with SPD might have in each category.

Sight

Children who have visual sensitivities might have issues with bright light. They might be extra sensitive to the sun and want to wear sunglasses or stay in the shade. You will see them squinting or turning their head away from the light. They might get visually distracted and have a hard time attending to tasks in front of them. Crowds might visually overwhelm them and make them feel nauseous.

Sounds

Children with auditory sensitivities might get overwhelmed by common household noises such as the flushing of the toilet, the noise of the washer and dryer, or the distant sound of a garbage truck. Outside noises such as sirens or a barking dog can cause distress. Events like fireworks or concerts can be unbearable for these children. They have an acute sense of hearing and they may have a hard time tuning out noises and focusing on an activity in front of them.

Touch

This can be one of the most problematic issues. Children with tactile defensiveness are highly sensitive to touch. Issues with clothes can become a daily struggle. Clothes with tags or seams become unwearable. Rough fabric, like jeans, becomes intolerable. Underwear can be perceived as too tight or too loose and children will often pull at their underwear throughout the day. Usually, children with tactile defensiveness like to wear cotton clothes without collars. They prefer seamless socks, flip flops and crocs on their feet. Some children will wear one type of clothing and refuse to wear anything else. For instance, they will only wear shorts, even in the winter, or they will only wear long pants, even in the summer. Sometimes these children prefer to wear as little as possible and would rather be in their underwear when they are at home. Bumps and scrapes are felt on a more intense level and they have a hard time calming down after a fall or an injury. Forget about combing or washing their hair. These children complain when someone touches their head and scream when their nails are cut. They will wipe off wet kisses and, in general, might excessively wipe their mouth, creating a red mark on their upper or lower lip. These children do not like to get their hands dirty and generally avoid any type of messy play.

The hyposensitive child also has issues with touch, but they struggle with being understimulated. They have a high level of energy and are constantly seeking sensory input by running, jumping, twirling and bumping into things. They might go around licking things and may put inedible objects like dirt and rocks in their mouth. They might crave hard hugs and might unintentionally hurt others with their tight squeezes. They seek out messy play and like to get their hands dirty.

Smell

Children with an acute sense of smell might gag easily when exposed to certain odors. They might smell things that you cannot smell. They have a sharper memory of various odors and their memories are more closely associated with smells. They may refuse to go to certain places or to other people's

207

homes due to the odor there. They get overwhelmed with the smell of perfume or lotion and can detect noxious smells like cigarette smoke long before anyone else can.

Taste/texture

This can be the most concerning of all the sensory processing issues. Issues with taste and texture can cause serious feeding problems. Oral sensitivities can cause a lack of weight gain and can affect the overall health of the child. Children with oral sensitivities have issues with various textures. They may not like chewy textures and might prefer soft textures. They may only want to eat foods like macaroni and cheese that are softer to eat, or prefer foods like crackers and cookies that quickly crumble in their mouth. Children usually have issues with meats that don't quickly dissolve in their mouth and tend to be chewier. These children do not like mixed textures like yogurt with fruit or cottage cheese. They are sensitive to new tastes and are usually very picky eaters. They prefer bland or less flavorful foods. They usually can detect when you use a different brand of the same type of food and will insist that you stay with the same brand you always use. They might feel their food is too hot, even when it seems lukewarm to your touch.

Children with hyposensitivities to taste and texture have the opposite problem. They are less sensitive and tend to stuff their mouth until they look like a little chipmunk. They overfill their mouth when they are eating because they have a harder time feeling the food in their mouth. They prefer strong flavors and are more open to trying new and different foods. These children will often put things in their mouth to chew on. They will chew on toys and their fingers. They may also go around licking various inedible objects in their environment.

Movement and balance

Children who struggle with movement and balance may have sensory issues with their vestibular system. Children with hypersensitivities in this area struggle with simple rides, swings, playground bridges, roped jungle gyms, escalators and elevators. They suffer from motion sickness frequently and have a hard time with things that move (cars, planes and trains). They may feel sick if they go upside down and it can put them in a state of panic. They feel nauseous if they are riding backwards on something that is moving and will avoid most basic rides at amusement parks.

Conversely, the hyposensitive child is understimulated by movement, so therefore is constantly seeking it. These children love fast rides and they seek out constant stimulation. They love to be thrown up in the air or spun around. You will find this child jumping off the couch and twirling themselves round and round until they collapse. This child may appear fearless and has no problem climbing to the top of a jungle gym or balancing on top of a playground set.

Body position and muscle control

Children with body position and muscle control issues have sensory issues with their proprioceptive system. This system provides your child with feedback about their body's movement and position. Children who have struggles with their proprioceptive system can be construed as clumsy and uncoordinated. They might bump into things, have poor posture and low muscle tone. They may struggle with knowing how much pressure to use in various tasks such as drawing. They might scribble too hard and break crayons or they might draw too lightly so that it is hard to see their work. These children may have a difficult time knowing how much energy to use and might be too rough with other kids or might unintentionally break toys. They might be constantly chewing on things and can chew on their fingers until they bleed. They might appear floppy or seem to have low muscle control.

Sensory processing treatment

Many of you reading about sensory processing issues may have recognized symptoms not only in your child, but maybe in yourself. Most of us have degrees of hyper- and hyposensitivities that we have lived with without concern. For some children, it is only necessary to understand and define their sensory issues. At times, parents will inaccurately label sensory struggles as poor behavior. They might think that their child is actively being defiant or difficult when they do not eat the food they are given. They might think their child is being too controlling when they refuse to wear jeans. Once you know your child's behaviors are not intentional, you can approach the issue in a different manner. Treating sensory issues with discipline is not only ineffective, it can exacerbate the problem.

If your child's sensory processing issues are mild, you may be able to help them cope with their sensory sensitivities without further intervention. As I stated before, there are plenty of resources and books dedicated to the topic of parenting a child with SPD. If you feel your child's sensory struggles impede their social or emotional growth or impact on their daily functioning, you might want to get them assessed by an occupational therapist. There are occupational therapists who specialize in SPD and have specific therapies to address the needs of those children. They can also teach you approaches and exercises to do at home to help your child cope and adapt to their environment.

CHAPTER 12

Extreme Behaviors

Seeking out professional support is a personal decision. There are many parents who have the ability to utilize resources and educate themselves enough to work with their anxious child without additional support; others might find it beneficial to have a child therapist for extra support and guidance. There is no right or wrong decision. However, if your child is exhibiting more extreme behaviors, this may be an indication that they could benefit from early intervention. The more proactive parents are in getting their children help, the more promising the prognosis will be long term. I will outline some of the more clinically significant behaviors that should warrant professional intervention. It is best to not have a wait-and-see attitude when it comes to mental health. The earlier a child gets help, the better the outcome.

Extreme behaviors

You may not know what would constitute "extreme behavior" and that might leave you feeling unsettled. Below are some behaviors that should be further assessed by a mental health professional:

> › Pulls eyelashes, eyebrows or hair out.
> › Hits head on hard surface repeatedly.
> › Bites themselves and leaves marks.
> › Scratches themselves and leaves marks.
> › Bites nails until they bleed.
> › Refuses to talk to anyone except immediate family (completely mute).
> › Gets so nervous they break out in hives or throw up.
> › Has food issues causing weight loss or failure to thrive.
> › Makes no eye contact.
> › Spins objects or likes to rock back and forth.

This is not an exhaustive list and if you have any concerns, it would be beneficial to talk to your pediatrician or a mental health provider for further guidance.

Keeping an eye on the future

Anxiety looks different at various stages of development. As children get older, their worries and anxieties shift and change. I will outline some of the more common worries children tend to have as they reach school age. There are also other issues and disorders that anxious children are more prone to encounter as they get older. It is helpful to arm yourself with the knowledge of what anxiety looks like as your child moves through different developmental stages. Of course, not every anxious toddler will continue to have anxiety, but knowing what to look for will help to ensure that early signs are not missed. Below is a brief snapshot of some common anxiety-related disorders.

Generalized Anxiety Disorder

When children get older, they tend to get anxious and perseverate on different themes to those that preoccupied them as toddlers. When a child continually worries and becomes irritable and distracted based on these worries, they may have Generalized Anxiety Disorder (GAD). Some common anxieties might center on a fear of:

> fire starting in the home

> people breaking into their home

> getting kidnapped or being hurt by a stranger

> ghosts, zombies or aliens hurting them

> dolls, puppets, clowns coming alive and hurting them

> storms and weather

> the world ending (sun exploding, an asteroid hitting the earth)

> something bad happening to the ones they love

> getting sick or having a disease

> social situations

> failing (can't make any errors academically or athletically)

> not looking perfect and acting perfectly

> disappointment (need to be a people pleaser)

> bugs, bees, birds, dogs and other living things that can harm them.

When your child's fears or phobias affect their social, educational or emotional well-being, it is time to get some professional help. When in doubt, have your child assessed by a pediatrician or mental health provider. Talk to your child's teachers to get additional information on how they are acting in various environments. Sometimes anxiety symptoms are only shown at home or at school. If your child is having a hard time sleeping or has stomach aches that have no medical origin, these could be signs of possible anxiety.

Obsessive Compulsive Disorder

Obsessive compulsive behaviors do not usually evolve until a child is school aged or older. Obsessive Compulsive Disorder (OCD) is characterized by compulsive behavior driven by an obsessive thought. Often children will hide these type of behaviors and their OCD may go unnoticed for an extended period of time. OCD is a complicated disorder because it can look vastly different in each child. Some typical obsessions may include, but are not limited to, these type of concerns:

> Having contact with urine or feces.

> Getting sick from germs.

> Getting poisoned by household cleaners, markers or other objects.

> Hurting themselves or hurting someone else.

> Having "bad" thoughts.

> Inadvertently cheating on a test.

> Having a bad thought about someone else.

> Having gay or inappropriate sexual thoughts that disturb them.

> Upsetting God or having thoughts that they think are immoral.

> Feeling things are uneven or unfair.

> Thinking something bad is going to happen to themselves or to someone they love.

> Forgetting something (to do homework, locking doors, turning things off).

When children have these invasive thoughts they feel a great deal of stress. Even though they may intellectually realize that their thoughts are irrational, they continue to bring them intense anxiety. When children have OCD, they find brief relief by doing compulsive actions. These actions look different for each child and therefore can be hard to detect initially. Some children try to conceal their compulsive rituals so that other people won't notice. Below are some common compulsive behaviors:

> Washes hands often or for an extended period of time.

> Constantly changes underwear or clothes due to belief they have got urine or feces on them.

> Won't touch doors, handles or light switches (sometimes uses elbows or their shirt).

> Has to do things evenly (if they hit one side of their body, they have to hit the other side).

> Does things a certain number of times (usually has a favorite number or even/odds).

> Has to redo things until it feels "right."

> Has a ritual to ward off "bad thoughts" (a bodily ritual that can look like a tic).

> Constantly checks behavior (checks for doors being locked, rechecks backpack).

> Will not touch things they feel are "contaminated" (avoids rooms, items, chairs).

> Needs to avoid walking in/on certain areas because something bad will happen.

> Says something to undo a bad thought or word.

> Confesses to another (usually a parent) about their bad thoughts.

> Arranges things in a certain order until it feels "right."

Obviously these lists are not exhaustive, but it should give you an idea of what type of themes may come up when your child is struggling with OCD behavior. If your child starts to exhibit some of these behaviors, discuss it with a pediatrician or mental health provider. It is better to be overly cautious and get your child assessed early if you have any concerns.

Separation Anxiety Disorder

Most parents believe that separation anxiety occurs when a child is a toddler, but what many people do not realize is that *clinical* separation anxiety usually occurs when a child is school aged. Clinical separation anxiety can manifest after a life-changing event or when a child transitions to middle school. Frequently there is no trigger that causes it, but commonly the first sign of clinical separation anxiety is a child frequently complaining of feeling sick. Children will complain of headaches and stomach aches on school days and on Sunday nights. Often these children are taken to pediatricians and gastrointestinal specialists where no medical origin is discovered. Most children will deny having any anxiety or stress related to school. Children may tell their parents, "I just want to stay at home" or "I feel more comfortable at home." Parents will sometimes think their child is being bullied or that there is some other stressor happening at school. These children will often aggressively refuse to go to school and will become uncharacteristically obstinate and oppositional.

Children with clinical separation anxiety are typically fearful that something bad will happen to them or to their parent (usually their mother) if they are not together. They develop an irrational belief that they and their parent are only safe if they are together. These children will sometimes worry that they will get sick and throw up if they are not with their parent. They will often make repeated trips to the nurse and are initially sent home on a regular basis due to a stomach ache or headache. Once a child is back at home with their parent, their physical symptoms disappear.

When a child shows symptoms of Separation Anxiety Disorder, it is important not to allow your child to stay at home. When a child is allowed to be avoidant, their anxiety increases and the disorder becomes more acute. The first step is to rule out any medical origin. Once a medical origin has been ruled out, it is helpful to talk to your child's school counselor (if they have one) or their teacher. Developing a plan with the school on how to approach your child's separation anxiety will be key to long-term success. As with any of these disorders, it is helpful to get the support of a mental health professional.

Selective mutism

Selective mutism is often dismissed as just "shyness" and can go undetected until the child enters kindergarten or first grade when the school voices concern over why the child is not talking. Children with selective mutism are completely mute in certain social situations, while not having any issues with talking in other situations. It is common for a child with selective mutism to talk normally at home and to be completely mute at school. Some children prefer to talk to only a select group of people whom they feel completely comfortable around. If your child is completely non-verbal in some social situations or continues to be completely silent after the first month of school, you might want to have them assessed. The school can be a wonderful source of services and support. Children with selective mutism can benefit from speech therapy and school accommodations for improved learning.

Panic attacks

Children who have panic attacks experience a number of physical symptoms. They may feel as if their heart is racing or that it is pounding in their chest. They may become sweaty, dizzy and nauseous or feel out of breath. Some children are fearful they are dying or think they are losing control. They might have feelings of depersonalization where they feel detached from themselves and are in a dream-like state. Usually panic attacks last less than an hour and may occur daily or monthly. Children who have panic attacks become anxious about when and where they will have their next attack. They may refuse to go to school or, in acute situations, refuse to leave the house due to their fear of another attack. Some children feel safest when they are close to their mom and come to the irrational conclusion that if they are with their parent, they will not have panic attacks. Children with panic attacks would benefit from ongoing therapy to learn coping mechanisms and relaxation techniques and should be assessed by a mental health practitioner.

Hair pulling (trichotillomania) and picking disorder

It is not uncommon for hair pulling and picking behavior to be misunderstood by parents. Some parents don't realize that pulling out one's hair or picking at a scab incessantly is a mental health issue.

Hair pulling, also known as trichotillomania, occurs when a child has the urge to pull out hair. Children will most often pull hair from their scalp, eyebrows and eyelashes. This behavior can go unnoticed until bald patches appear, or eyebrows or eyelashes are almost completely gone. Children with anxiety are at a higher risk of these type of behaviors.

Picking at scabs repeatedly is not only a medical concern but can be a mental health issue as well. The urge to continually pick your skin can be very strong and children can have a difficult time fighting it. This can become more of a concern when the scabs get infected or start to leave scarring on the body.

Both hair pulling and skin picking can be treated through therapy. If you notice your child is pulling out large amounts of their hair or their scabs are being picked to the point of possible infection, it is time to get them assessed by a mental health provider.

Conclusion: Looking into the Future

It is important to remember that children are resilient and adaptable. Even though your child may have anxiety, you can teach them the skills and coping mechanisms to have a happy, healthy, productive life. When your child is exhibiting some disturbing or confusing behavior, it can be overwhelming and, ironically, anxiety-producing. The important thing to remember is that children can be taught how to fight their fears and overcome much of their anxiety. Parents who react calmly and do not add their own ingredient of anxiety to the mix help by being their child's anchor. When your child is feeling panicked and nervous, don't bring your own nervous energy to the situation. Tether your child's feelings of instability by being their rock.

There are things you can control and there are things you cannot control. Once you realize that, you can pour your attention into the areas where you can make the most difference. You cannot own your child's anxiety or you will both drown. You cannot take your child's fears away, but you can empower your child to fight them. You cannot stop your child from worrying, but you can teach them alternative ways of thinking. You cannot take your child's sensory issues away, but you can help them adapt to their environment.

The most important thing to remember is the more you accommodate and enable your child's anxiety, the longer it will be around. Take your child's lead and know when to push and when to hug. Helping your child get rid of their anxiety is not a sprint, but a marathon. An over-zealous parent can exacerbate their child's anxiety. Find your child's pace and match it. Balance is key. Remember, this is your child's anxiety and you are only a guide and a support for them through this process.

Index